To my little ♡ Boy
on his 40TH!

OL DAD

A NICE LITTLE PLACE ON THE

NORTH SIDE

A NICE LITTLE PLACE ON THE
NORTH SIDE

WRIGLEY FIELD AT ONE HUNDRED

GEORGE F. WILL

CROWN
ARCHETYPE

New York

Copyright © 2014 by George F. Will

All rights reserved.
Published in the United States by Crown Archetype, an imprint of
the Crown Publishing Group, a division of Random House LLC,
a Penguin Random House Company, New York.
www.crownpublishing.com

Crown Archetype with colophon is a trademark of Random House
LLC.

Text credits appear on pages 215–216.
Photo credits appear on page 217.

Library of Congress Cataloging-in-Publication Data
Will, George F.
A nice little place on the North Side : Wrigley Field at one hundred /
George F. Will.
   pages cm
1. Wrigley Field (Chicago, Ill.)—History. 2. Chicago Cubs (Baseball
team)—History. I. Title.
 GV417.W75W55 2014
 796.357068773'11—dc23
 2013036084

ISBN 978-0-385-34931-4
eBook ISBN 978-0-385-34932-1

Printed in the United States of America

Ivy illustration by Fred Haynes
Jacket photographs: Victoria Will (front), Chase Swift/Corbis
Images (back)

10 9 8 7 6 5 4 3 2 1

First Edition

TO BUD

AND SUE SELIG

Architecture is inhabited sculpture.

—CONSTANTIN BRANCUSI

Acknowledgments

My assistant Sarah Walton is She Who Must Be Obeyed, not because she is imperious but because she is infallible. Helping with the preparation of this book has quickened her interest in baseball but diminished her affection for the Chicago Cubs. A good exchange. Todd Shaw, my research assistant, brought to the elimination of errors in this book a perfectionism rarely seen on the diamond at Wrigley Field.

On June 20, 1941, the poet Robert Frost, then sixty-seven, recited for the first time in public his poem "The Lesson for Today." Its last line is perhaps his most famous:

> I would have written of me on my stone:
> I had a lover's quarrel with the world.

Frost died in 1963, and this line is carved on the headstone of his grave in Bennington, Vermont. My lover's quarrel is less spacious than Frost's. Mine is with the Chicago National League Ball Club. The world is what it is and has been very good to me. The Cubs, however, are another matter. They have been generally disappointing and often annoying for most of my life, which began forty-seven days before Frost announced his quarrel. Why, then, have I, like many millions of similarly vexed and irritated fans, continued to love this team? There are, no doubt, many reasons. Or, because reason rarely regulates love, let us say there are many factors that explain the durability of my affection, and that of others, for the Cubs. Surely the most important ingredient in the chemistry of this peculiar loyalty is the place where the team has played its home games for a century. Wrigley Field really is a nice little place. Granted, few people would care about it if the Cubs did not play there. But a lot fewer people would care about the Cubs if they did not play there. What follows is a short stroll through the braided histories of the place and the team, both of which are facets of one of America's singular cities. I will begin with my beginning.

I was born on Sunday morning, May 4, 1941, in Champaign, Illinois. The *Chicago Tribune* that morning reported that on Saturday the Cubs had been "characteristically docile" through the first five innings while losing to the Brooklyn Dodgers, 4–3, in Ebbets Field. On Sunday the Cubs crossed the East River and lost to the New York Giants, 9–4. It was their third loss in a row. Had I been paying attention then, this book might not have been written. But one thing led to another, as things have a way of doing, and in 1948, when I was still not as discerning as one should be when making life-shaping decisions, I became a Cub fan. The Catholic Church thinks seven-year-olds have reached an age of reasoning. The church might want to rethink that.

The 1948 Cubs may have been the worst squad in the history of the franchise, finishing in eighth place—which in those days was last place—and 27½ games out of first. The dreadful team inspired a Norman Rockwell cover on the September 4 *Saturday Evening Post*. Titled *The Dugout*, it featured a dejected and embarrassed Cubs dugout, behind which fans jeered. Their well-named manager was Charlie Grimm. He was, however, known as "Jolly Cholly" Grimm because he was so cheerful. Why was he?

On August 30, 1948, the Cubs' owner, Philip K. Wrigley, ran an ad in the *Tribune*, which thirty-three years later would buy the Cubs from Wrigley's estate, to apologize for the team. The ad told the unvarnished truth: "This year's rebuilding job has been a flop." You might say that. The last-place Cubs' record was 64–90. The 1940s, my first decade, was the first losing decade the Cubs ever had. Since then, the Cubs have not had a winning decade. Since May 4, 1941, and through the 2013 season, they have lost 693 more games than they have won. What could compensate Cub fans for such a performance on the field? The field. Wrigley Field. This little book is about a little space. It is not, regardless of what some unhinged enthusiasts say, a sacred space. Wrigley Field's footprint on a city block is a tad smaller than that of St. Peter's Basilica in Rome. The enthusiasts think the ballpark is a kind of cathedral, and that Wrigley Field is to baseball what Rome is, or was once said to be, to religion: All roads lead there, or should.

This book is, in a sense, about a frame around a picture. The point of Wrigley Field is to display baseball games. People go to museums of fine art to see the paintings, not the frames that display them. Few people admire the pedestal more than the statue. Many people do, however, decide to go to Chicago Cubs games because they are played within this lovely frame. And just as a frame can serve, or be inappropriate for, a particular painting, ballparks can display ball games well or poorly. It is frequently noted that Wrigley Field is lovelier than the baseball often played on the field. It is a hypothesis of this book that the ballpark is part cause and part symptom of the Cubs' dysfunctional performance. How can this high-quality building be partly responsible for the low quality of what has gone on in it? Read on.

The story of the ballpark is braided with the story of the baseball team, and of a city. The ballpark has not been merely a passive ingredient in the Cubs' story. It has shaped what it has framed. And if architecture is inhabited sculpture, Wrigley Field has shaped the scores of millions who have, episodically and briefly, inhabited it. Ernest Dimnet was a French abbé who frequently traveled and lectured in the United States. His business was soul, and he said: "Architecture, of all the arts, is the one which acts the most slowly, but the most surely, on the soul." This is perhaps especially true of architecture that does not set out to work upon the soul—architecture that is unself-consciously utilitarian, as Wrigley Field is. It has been well said that architecture exists not for the structure itself but for the space the structure creates by enclosing it. The space Wrigley Field encloses—the playing field—created Wrigley Field. Because space dictated the configuration of the building, it can be said that baseball built it. Which is why people care about the corner of Clark and Addison Streets.

The home plate entrance to Wrigley is at that corner. Clark, along the third-base side of the ballpark, is named for General George Rogers Clark, the son of Virginia landowners, who at age twenty went west in search of land and adventure, finding much of both. He distinguished himself in the Revolutionary War by projecting the new

A highlight of the Cubs' first year at Clark and Addison.

nation's power into what became the Northwest Territory, including the state of Illinois.

It is known that, but not why, Addison Street, along the first-base side of Wrigley Field, is named for Dr. Thomas Addison of Guy's Hospital in London. He identified a form of anemia that now bears his name—Addisonian anemia. Please, let there be no tart remarks about the appropriateness, over the last half century, of the Cubs being associated with the anemic. Additionally, Addison's anemia is not Addison's disease, which afflicted John F. Kennedy.

Balls hit over the right-field wall land on Sheffield Avenue, named for Joseph E. Sheffield, a go-getter who, like many who made the Northwest Territory prosper, came from New England—from Connecticut. In the 1830s, he started a farm and nursery and bought some of the land that became the Lincoln Park neighborhood on the North Side, about halfway between what now is the Loop to the south and Wrigley Field to the north. But the basis of Sheffield's wealth was the business that made Chicago boom: railroads. Sheffield was a founder of the Chicago, Rock Island and Pacific Railroad and a builder of the New Haven and Northampton Railroad back in Connecticut. By 1914, many railroads were bringing people, and the produce of the prairies, to Chicago.

Balls hit over Wrigley Field's left-field wall land on Waveland Avenue. This name was chosen by Sheffield, the developer and subdivider, because on stormy days some of his land on the portion of the avenue near Lake Michigan was inundated.

There are no waves in central Illinois. There the land is flat, so some people consider the vistas dull. But, then, there are those who consider baseball dull, and as sportscaster Red Barber once said, baseball is dull only to dull minds. The highest hill in Champaign County is not much more than a pitcher's mound, but it's quite high enough. The vast spaces of America's Great Plains are well configured for endless baseball diamonds, with foul lines extending to far horizons. Thanks to the slow work of glaciers over many millennia, much of the land of central Illinois is astonishingly black, fertile, and valuable. It is also heavy, and for the first farmers who settled there, it was very difficult to plow. But in the 1830s, in the village of Grand Detour, a young blacksmith took up the challenge of designing a self-scouring steel plow to turn the heavy soil. He succeeded, and today his name is on big green machines all over the world: John Deere. And on little green machines, like the riding mowers that trim suburban lawns. And urban infields and outfields.

The twin cities of Champaign and Urbana are the home of one of the main branches of the University of Illinois, where for thirty-seven years my father was a professor of philosophy. One of his interests was the concept of probability, concerning which he tried to tutor me, using Cubs players like Roy Smalley. Smalley was the Cubs' shortstop from the fateful 1948 season through 1953. His career batting average was .227. He would come to the plate batting about that, and the Cubs' radio announcer Bert Wilson would cheerfully say, "Smalley is overdue for a hot streak." My father would patiently explain to me that Stan Musial batting .227—not that he ever did that—would be overdue but that Smalley was just being himself. In 1950, Smalley did, however, lead the league in two categories: He struck out 114 times and made 51 errors. So, fifty-one times that season the shortstop, the most important defensive player in fair territory (that is, excluding the catcher), gave a major league opponent an extra out in an inning. It is a wonder the 1950 Cubs managed to finish only 26½ games out of first place. I should have paid more attention to logic, but Cub fans obviously don't. The Cubs do, however, make many of their fans philosophical, as *Merriam-Webster's Collegiate Dictionary* defines that: "calm or unflinching in the face of trouble, defeat, or loss."

Champaign and Urbana are cheek by jowl because of the Illinois Central Railroad. It is mostly gone, a victim of a merger and the disappearing railroad blues, but once it was so mighty it moved towns. When the first passenger train arrived in the area, in 1854, it came on tracks laid two miles west of the Champaign County Courthouse, in Urbana—a courthouse in which some cases had been argued by a canny and successful, hence prosperous, railroad lawyer named Abraham Lincoln. The land west of Urbana was cheaper, and the town of West Urbana grew up around the tracks. Soon Urbana tried to incorporate the upstart town, but the upstart had acquired, as upstarts will do, pride. It asserted its independence and took the name Champaign. So it became the stopping point for evocatively named passenger trains—the Panama Limited, the City of New Orleans, the City of Miami, and the Seminole. They steamed, and then were diesel-drawn, from the Deep South to Chicago.

Back in what are now regarded as the Dark Ages of Parenting, before Baby Boomer parents made their original discovery that the world has sharp edges and abrasive surfaces, before society achieved today's degree of pitiless enlightenment and decided that children should be enveloped in bubble wrap, like Dresden porcelain, lest they get chipped or otherwise damaged, and forced to wear crash helmets, back then we, the potentially lost youth of central Illinois, would ride our balloon-tire Schwinn bikes down to the railroad tracks and amuse ourselves by clambering over the boxcars on sidings while trains rumbled past nearby. All the while, we thought of the destination of the north-bound trains: Chicago.

It certainly is natural and probably is healthy for young people in small communities to have metropolitan yearn-ings. Many such yearnings have been directed east, toward New York. Mine were directed north, toward Chicago, for two reasons. One reason was those passenger trains, which seemed drawn with their riders to Chicago, as iron filings are drawn to a magnet, by an invisible force. The other reason was radio, by which Chicago reached out to inform, entertain, and entice. For this downstate Illinois boy, the railroad pointed toward a destination from which the most interesting radio broadcasts originated: Wrigley Field.

Baseball fans, an otherwise sensible and agreeable co-hort, are given to gushing. It is a grating attribute. Many people in this modern age are relentless in sharing their feelings about this and that, and baseball fans can be es-pecially so. They have a high-octane sentimentality about everything from playing catch with Dad to baseball's re-semblance to heaven—how *do* they know?—or Pericles's Athens, or the Federal Reserve Board. Is there anything that baseball has *not* been said to resemble? Or to be a metaphor for? And the gushing is never worse than when Cub fans get going about Wrigley Field. It is, they think, if thinking can be said to enter into such talk, a little fore-taste of—you guessed it—the hereafter. The only real resemblance between Wrigley Field and heaven is that the ballpark is indeed the final destination of some Cub fans. Every once in a while someone in the bleachers leans out from the front row and, pursuant to the wishes of the deceased, pours onto the outfield a small billowing gray cloud of dust that is the ashes of Uncle Ralph or Aunt Min, who, one hopes, really meant it when he or she said, "You know, when I die I wish . . ." This use of Wrigley Field is officially frowned upon, but it is believably said, *sotto voce*, that ushers and other representatives of officialdom have been known to enable this by pretending not to see it.

Never mind that before this heavenly place on the North Side could be built, a Lutheran seminary had to be torn down. Or that the Chicago National League Ball Club wanted to evict the Lutherans so it could escape a neighborhood that contained too many people who were, well, just not the right sort, if you get my drift—immigrants and other members of the lower orders. Never mind, too, that those neighbors included a secular saint of American history: Jane Addams, the founder of Hull House, where you might encounter young idealists destined for greatness.

One such who worked at Hull House was a New Yorker, Frances Perkins, a social reformer whose zeal, already hot, had been further quickened on March 25, 1911. She had been taking tea in the heart of Manhattan, near the Triangle Shirtwaist factory, when it caught fire. The blaze killed 146 workers, mostly young immigrant women trapped by locked doors, and ignited a new era of government regulations to improve conditions for working people. Perkins became President Franklin Roosevelt's secretary of labor—America's first female member of a president's cabinet.

Another person whose ascent to greatness included time spent at Hull House was Paul Douglas. In 1920, at age twenty-eight, he became a professor of industrial relations at the University of Chicago, which he left in 1942 to enlist as a fifty-year-old private in the Marine Corps, rising to the rank of lieutenant colonel. He was elected to the U.S. Senate in 1948, for the first of three terms. He, too, lived in the neighborhood the Cubs fled in 1914.

Chicago has a rich history of remarkable people. It also has a deserved reputation as a tough town. Wrigley Field is a green and pleasant jewel that was set, one hundred years ago, in a city with dark, satanic aspects.

If Chicago, a no-nonsense city of prose, ever had a poet, it was, of course, Carl Sandburg. Since his death in 1967, at age eighty-nine, his reputation has fallen on hard times, and has fallen from quite a height. In the 1950s and 1960s, he was what now seems like an oxymoron, a celebrity poet. He appeared on *The Ed Sullivan Show*—after Elvis but before the Beatles—and the *Today* show with Dave Garroway, and *Texaco Star Theater* with the comedian Milton Berle, and he was interviewed by the high priest of broadcast journalism, Edward R. Murrow. It is, however, safe to say that almost no one reads Sandburg anymore, and he has become the object of withering witticisms. Clichés, wrote the essayist Joseph Epstein, run through Sandburg's writing like calories through cheesecake. Of Sandburg's thick and weird "biography" of Abraham Lincoln—no citations, just unoriginal narrative laced with Sandburg's musings—Edmund Wilson said, "There are moments when one is tempted to feel that the cruelest thing that has happened to Lincoln since he was shot by Booth has been to fall into the hands of Carl Sandburg." Sandburg's brother-in-law was the photographer Edward Steichen, who said that when God created Sandburg, He did not do anything else that day. Others have said that perhaps He thought he had done enough damage for one day. And yet.

Sandburg helped bring poetry out from the parlor with the white curtains and into the streets that churned up the urban grime that soiled the white curtains that were "white prayers" for gentility in an industrial world:

> Dust and the thundering trucks won—the
> barrages of the street wheels and the
> lawless wind took their way—was it five
> weeks or six the little mother, the new
> neighbors, battled and then took away the
> white prayers in the windows?

Sandburg's *Chicago Poems*, published in 1916, the year the Cubs moved into what would come to be called Wrigley Field, contain his most famous lines:

> Hog Butcher for the World,
> Tool Maker, Stacker of Wheat,

> Player with Railroads and the Nation's Freight
> Handler,
> Stormy, husky, brawling,
> City of the Big Shoulders.

Turning, however, from this celebratory tone, he wrote an indictment that begins:

> They tell me you are wicked and I believe
> them . . .

Then, turning again "to those who sneer at this my city," at this "tall bold slugger set vivid against the little soft cities," he says:

> Come and show me another city with lifted head
> singing so proud to be alive and coarse and
> strong and cunning.

When Frank Algernon Cowperwood, the cunning protagonist of Theodore Dreiser's boisterous Chicago novel *The Titan*, emerges, as he does in the book's first paragraph, from the Eastern District Penitentiary in Philadelphia, he heads for Chicago, where, Dreiser wrote, thirty railroads terminated, "as though it were the end of the world." Cowperwood arrived in something made there—a Pullman car produced by the Pullman Palace Car Company of George Mortimer Pullman. He owned the town of Pullman, which has long since been absorbed by Chicago's sprawl.

Chicago was just the place for a man with Cowperwood's high ratio of energy to scruples. As his train approached Chicago, he saw "here and there, a lone workingman's cottage, the home of some adventurous soul who had planted his bare hut thus far out in order to reap the small but certain advantage that the growth of the city would bring." "Seething" Chicago, with its "snap," its "swirling, increasing life," and its "tang of the future," convinced Dreiser—as it had convinced Henry Adams at the city's 1893 Columbian Exposition—that "the world was young here. Life was doing something new." Adams, as he famously recorded in *The Education of Henry Adams*, recoiled in dismay from this something new. Cowperwood embraced it. As did Dreiser, who was stirred by Chicago to some seriously overwrought sentences:

> This singing flame of a city, this all America, this poet in chaps and buckskin, this rude, raw Titan. . . . By its shimmering lake it lay, a king of shreds and patches, a maundering yokel with an epic in its mouth, a tramp, a hobo among cities, with the grip of Caesar in its mind, the dramatic force of Euripides in its soul. A very bard of a city this, singing of high deeds and high hopes, its heavy brogans buried deep in the mire of circumstance. . . . Here hungry men, raw from the shops and fields, idyls and romances in their minds, builded them an empire crying glory in the mud.

Good grief. Sandburg was pithier: "Here's the difference between us and Dante: He wrote a lot about Hell and never saw the place. We're writing about Chicago after looking the town over."

Long before Carl Sandburg called Chicago the city of the big shoulders, it was a city of clenched fists. Today, Wrigley Field is called—it is written on the roof of the visiting team's dugout—"the Friendly Confines." In 1914, the year *The Titan* was published, "friendly" was not the first adjective Chicago called to mind. And of queasy stomachs and an uneasy conscience: When, in 1906, Upton Sinclair's novel *The Jungle* depicted the immigrants' living and working conditions in and around the stockyards and meatpacking plants on Chicago's South Side, food safety became a federal issue.

Chicago was no stranger to the rawest aspects of this process of accommodation. In 1886, in the city's Haymarket Square, at a rally of fifteen hundred men and women demanding an eight-hour day, a bomb exploded, killing eleven, including seven policemen, and injuring one hundred. Consider the impression Chicago made on an impressionable eighteen-year-old from Morton, Illinois, in 1917, the year after the Cubs moved into Wrigley Field. David Lilienthal would, in his long public career, serve Wisconsin's Governor Philip La Follette on that state's public service commission, would serve President Franklin Roosevelt as a director of the Tennessee Valley Authority, and would serve President Truman as chairman of the

Atomic Energy Commission. The journal he kept throughout his life contains an entry for July 31, 1917, concerning "one of the most disgusting things I have ever witnessed":

> It had rained violently the day before, and here and there were large puddles of water, which had collected in the low places of the street. Around one of these puddles a large group of men had gathered. I noticed them from a distance—men of all classes, some in Palm Beach suits, others in stylish tailor-mades, and a few messenger boys and errand boys. A cab was standing in the puddle also, so I thought this was what had attracted the crowd. I stepped through the throng and was both surprised and shocked to see what these busy men-of-the-world were watching with such evident enjoyment was but a tiny mouse, swimming around in the pool. Whenever he would struggle to a place of safety—a clump of mud, perhaps—someone would stick out his mahogany cane and throw the poor quivering thing back to its death. When this would happen some portly comfortable-looking son-of-a-gun would shift his cigar and chuckle!

A toddling town, indeed. And one much in need of some friendly confines. But life in the early twentieth century was still rough and raw. The late Julian Simon, an economist, noted that back then "most people in the

United States died of environmental pollution—that is, from infectious diseases such as pneumonia, tuberculosis, and gastroenteritis." Healthy people—who might more accurately have been said to be relatively and temporarily healthy—took arduous and hazardous treks across the city to jobs where they worked long, hard, and dangerous days. So they seized their pleasures where they could. Beginning in 1914, many came to the ballpark on the North Side.

The history of the Cubs includes several remarkable continuities. Pat Pieper was the Wrigley Field public address announcer from the year the Cubs began playing there, 1916, until his death in 1974, at age eighty-eight. Yosh Kawano tended to the Cubs' clubhouse from 1943 through the 2007 season. The Cubs' story also includes many remarkable oddities.

The Cubs have been beaten by the Pirates 15–0 (1929) and 22–0 (1975), the latter being the most lopsided shutout in major league history, until matched by the Indians' 22–0 defeat of the Yankees on August 31, 2004. Although the Cubs won the pennant in 1938, their pitcher Larry French managed to lose nineteen games—almost a third of the team's sixty-three losses. Lou "the Mad Russian" Novikoff, who played for the wartime Cubs from 1941 through 1944, once tried to steal third *with the bases loaded* because "I got such a good jump on the pitcher." On September 13, 1942, shortstop Lennie Merullo committed four errors *in one inning*. A son was born to him that day, and he named him Boots. Two Cubs catchers, George Mitterwald in 1974 and Barry Foote in 1980, each had a game in which they drove in eight runs. And each ended their respective seasons with just twenty-eight RBIs. On September 1, 1961, another Cubs catcher, Cuno Barragan, hit a home run in his first major league at bat. He never hit another. In one period of eleven years, the Cubs had no twenty-game winners but three twenty-game losers (Bob Rush in 1950, Sam Jones in 1955, and Glen Hobbie in 1960).

On May 2, 1956, Cubs third baseman Don Hoak tied a major league batting record. Unfortunately, he did it by striking out six times in an extra-inning (seventeen-inning) game. In 1968, Cubs pitcher Bill Hands recorded fourteen consecutive strikeouts. Regrettably, he did this as a batter in consecutive at bats. On September 16, 1972, Cubs second baseman Glenn Beckert set a major league batting record by stranding twelve base runners in a nine-inning game. In each of two innings, the third and the seventh, he stranded four. On August 14, 1979, Cubs right fielder Mike Vail, trying to throw a runner out at the plate, beaned the batboy. Vail was charged with two errors on the play, one for dropping the ball while fielding it and another for the wild throw that hit the batboy. On June 30, 1979, the Cubs tied a major league record by scoring five runs in the bottom of the eleventh inning. Unfortunately, they lost to the

Mets, who had scored six in the top of the inning. Think about that.

The Cubs have often been jokes, and have given rise to more than a few, such as: What does a female bear taking birth control pills have in common with the World Series? No Cubs. And: For most teams, 0 for 30 is called a calamity. For the Cubs, it is called April. The Cubs' last World Series victory was in 1908, so in a sense this book is being published in the 106th year of the Cubs' rebuilding effort. Cub fans like to say that any team can have a bad century, but the Cubs have a winless streak older than its century-old ballpark. Still, there is glory to be found if you look back far enough.

The Cubs' pre-Wrigley record was 1,219 wins and 754 losses, a nifty 465 games over .500. The 1906–1910 Cubs had the highest five-season winning percentage (.693) in baseball history. The second highest? The Cubs 1905–1909 (.678). Third highest? The Cubs 1904–1908 (.664). From 1948 through the 96-loss 2013 season, the Cubs have won 4,871 times and lost 5,564 times. Thus from 1948—encompassing Truman's defeat of Dewey, the Marshall Plan, and the reelection of Chicago's Barack Obama as president—through 2013, they were 693 games under .500, with a winning percentage of .467.

So, before the Cubs moved into Wrigley, they were what the New York Yankees were to become: a byword for excellence. But from 1940, when the Cubs had their first losing record (75–79) in fifteen years, through 1966—from before Pearl Harbor, through the Korean War, and during the escalation in Vietnam—the Cubs had just three winning seasons. In the best of them, in 1945, the Cubs won the pennant and took the Tigers to the seventh game of the World Series before losing. It is, however, hard for Cub fans to take much pleasure from this tainted glory because the war had thoroughly depleted major league talent. The Cardinals had dominated the first half of the decade; they won the National League pennant in 1942, 1943, and 1944, and won the 1942 and 1944 World Series. In 1945, however, they lost Stan Musial to the navy. How important was that? When Eddie Sawyer, who managed the Phillies after the war, was asked about the best team he had ever seen, he answered: "Musial." In 1946, Musial returned and the Cubs came back to earth, winning sixteen fewer games (82–71).

Since moving into Wrigley Field, the Cubs' most successful stretch was winning four pennants in ten seasons, from 1929 through 1938. Beginning in 1926, the team finished in what was then called the first division—fourth or better in the eight-team league—in fourteen consecutive seasons, winning ninety or more games in six of them. But from 1916, their first Wrigley Field season, through the 2013 season, their record was 7,478 and 7,833, a winning percentage of .488. They had just thirty-nine seasons with winning records. So, the franchise now called the Cubs had a long and often distinguished history, under various names, before the team moved into Wrigley Field.

Officially, the Cubs' story began in the nation's centennial year of 1876, but the preface to the story was written in 1870, when the White Stockings played a full season in, and won the championship of, a ramshackle league called the National Association of Base Ball Players. (Back then, "baseball" was still two words.) The White Stockings did not play in 1872 and 1873, because the city was still recovering from the fire supposedly caused by Mrs. O'Leary's cow kicking over the lantern. In 1876, however, Chicago pretty much invented what has become Major League Baseball.

In his book *Wrigleyville: A Magical History Tour of the Chicago Cubs*, Peter Golenbock, a versatile sportswriter with a flair for oral history, notes that Chicago gave the world such socially transformative developments as the skyscraper, the refrigerated railroad car, the meatpacking plant, and, when Richard Warren Sears met Alvah Curtis Roebuck in Chicago, the mail-order store. Chicago also pioneered the first professional baseball league. This was a start-up by a good ballplayer who was an even better entrepreneur.

Albert Goodwill Spalding, who did not always live up to his middle name, hailed from Rockford, Illinois, ninety miles west of Chicago. He broke Boston's heart by exercising a right he would be instrumental in denying to other players for another century. "Boston is mourning," reported a Boston newspaper on July 24, 1875. "Like Rachel weeping for her children, she refuses to be comforted because the famous baseball nine, the perennial champion, the city's most cherished possession, has been captured by

Chicago." Spalding and three other members of the Boston Red Stockings had behaved as what would later be
called "free agents," selling their services to the buyer they
preferred.

William Hulbert, a Chicago coal merchant who also
was president of the White Stockings, was, like his city,
on the rebound and on the make. A Chicago chauvinist,
he often said, "I'd rather be a lamppost in Chicago than
a millionaire in any other city." He laid down the law to
Spalding: "You've no business playing in Boston, you're a
Western boy and you belong right here." As Peter Levine
writes in A. G. *Spalding and the Rise of Baseball*, Bosto-
nians denounced the "dirty quartet of seceders"—a sting-
ing epithet just a decade after Appomattox—but Spalding
never looked back. In 1878, he became secretary of the
White Stockings and four years later was the team's owner
and president.

The constitution Spalding drafted for a new league, the
National League, which began in 1876, did not include a
reserve clause binding each player to his team until the
team chose to trade or release him. But such a clause was
added four years later. This denial of a fundamental right—
the right to sell one's labor to the highest bidder—would
not be rectified for a century, until in 1975 an arbitrator
overturned the reserve clause. In 1876, Spalding poached
from Philadelphia the first great star of what would become
the Cubs, Adrian "Cap" Anson, who played for Chicago
for twenty-two years and is in the Hall of Fame. Which is
in Cooperstown, New York, because Spalding, who was

not always fastidious about facts, fabricated the myth—announced in the 1908 *Spalding Guide*—that young Abner Doubleday invented baseball there one summer day in 1839 in Farmer Finney's pasture.

In 1876, Chicago's White Stockings, the mighty genesis of the Cubs, won the first National League pennant. Never one to let grass grow under his feet, Spalding retired as a player and began selling sporting goods. "One of his less successful ideas," Golenbock notes, "was that there be a different-colored uniform for each position. It was a brilliant suggestion for a man selling uniforms." That was not all Spalding sold. He became the official publisher of various official baseball guides, including the *National League Guide*. They contained all the official rules of baseball, one of which was that all league games had to use Spalding baseballs.

You might say that the Cubs franchise peaked a little early: Led by Cap Anson, the White Stockings won pennants in 1880, 1881, 1882, 1885, and 1886. He was called Cap Anson because there was altogether too much of his real name, which was Adrian Constantine Anson, an homage to two Michigan towns where his father spent, we can assume, a happy childhood. Anson was the first major leaguer to collect more than 3,000 hits (3,418), including two home runs on his last day, at age forty-five. Anson's adamant opposition to allow African Americans to compete was important in establishing the uncodified but real agreement that Major League Baseball would be for white players only. It is, therefore, particularly satisfying that the most popular player ever to call Wrigley Field home is a black man, Ernie Banks.

In 1882, the American Association was formed to compete with the National League, which it did by allowing something the National League forbade: the sale of beer in the ballparks. Chicago had a particular flair for sin, which worried Spalding. An 1889 editorial in the *Spalding Guide* said, "The two great obstacles in the way of success of the majority of professional ball players are wine and women. The saloon and the brothel are the evils of baseball at the present day." Golenbock notes that Chicago's shopping center for dissipations was a neighborhood called the Levee because southern gamblers were influential there: "Within the borders of a few blocks there were more than 200 brothels."

There are those who argue that because lights came late to Wrigley Field, and because the number of night games is still limited by a city ordinance, the performance of Cubs players has suffered. This is so because they have had too much time in the evenings to play in Wrigleyville's bars or, for decades, downtown on Rush Street. But long before any ballpark had lights, Spalding decided to have the Cubs do their spring training in Hot Springs, Arkansas, to cure the effects of "winter lushing." Or as one reporter put it, "to boil out the alcohol microbes." This was pursuant to Spalding's insistence that baseball exemplify "American Courage, Confidence, Combativeness; American Dash, Discipline, Determination; American Energy, Eagerness, Enthusiasm; American Pluck, Persistency, Per-

INDIVIDUAL PLAYER REPORT

DATE   July 28, 1953   SCOUT Hugh Wise

NAME IN FULL   Ernest Banks

CLUB K.C. Monarchs   LEAGUE Negro American

PLAYER'S HOME ADDRESS Dallas Texas   c/o K.C. Monarchs
K.C., Kansas

POSITION SS   AGE 22   WGT. 180   HGT. 6'1"   BATS R   THROWS R

PHYSICAL DESCRIPTION Very good proportions-strong arms.
Lithe - angular - trim good legs.

NATIONALITY   Negro American   DATE OF BIRTH

HITTING good   RUNNING good   FIELDING very good

POWER good plus   ARM quick - strong
very good   ATTITUDE very good

SPEED   CURVE   CHANGE

CONTROL   POISE   STAMINA

MARRIED yes   HABITS very good   HUSTLE good

IS PLAYER PROSPECT   Yes.

PLAYER'S STRENGTH Ability, all around, outstanding
arm and good hitter.

PLAYER'S WEAKNESS No outstanding weakness.   Slowed up on
injury.

PLAYER'S MILITARY STATUS   Has served 2 yrs.

HOW MANY GAMES OBSERVED? 10 in 1950. 3 in 1953.

WHAT CLASSIFICATION PLAY NOW? AAA   Can play now.
YEARS BEFORE MAJOR LG?

DATE GRADUATED(S) HIGH SCHOOL   June 1950 or 1949.

PREVIOUS PRO EXPERIENCE   No - has been with Monarchs.

BASEBALL HISTORY AND REMARKS Started at 19 with Monarchs,
played all of 1950. Military service in 51 and52
With Monarchs this year. Suffered right ankle
injury (sprained). Also had trouble with left
knee in Service but now healed. Recommend we
purchase up to $10,000.
(over)

BASEBALL SELECTION STATUS:

"Can play now." Indeed.

formance; American Spirit, Sagacity, Success; American Vim, Vigor, Virility."

Another short-lived rival of the National League was the Players' League, which included the Chicago Onions. That's an off-putting name—even worse than the Cleveland Spiders—but it's justified, sort of, by the fact that the name Chicago derives from a Native American word for a wild onion. Spalding solved this problem of a competitor team by buying 60 percent of it, which got him a ballpark and some players he melded with the White Stockings. Under the, shall we say, *relaxed* rules of the day, Spalding simultaneously owned stock in another White Stockings rival, the New York Giants.

By the time Spalding retired, in 1902, his team had a new owner, Jim Hart, and needed a new name. The team had been called the Colts, or Anson's Colts, until Anson's twenty-two years with the team ended. After his retirement, some newspapers had begun referring to the team as the Orphans. Because Hart signed so many young players, the team was briefly called the Spuds. This nomenclature chaos had to stop, but the team could not go back to being the White Stockings, because in 1902 the American League was formed and the name was grabbed by the team on Chicago's South Side. According to Golenbock, at about this time a group of Chicagoans recommended finding a name that would suggest "bear-like strength and a playful disposition." And one newspaper's sports editor began substituting "Cubs" for "Orphans" and "Spuds."

Soon the Cubs were generating big headlines. Beginning in 1904, the team had a future Hall of Fame pitcher,

Mordecai "Three Finger" Brown. He'd earned his nickname the hard way, by a common nineteenth-century hazard: an accident with a farm implement. The culprit was a corn shredder, against which Brown harbored no grudge: After his baseball career ended, he ran a service station in Terre Haute, Indiana, where customers could gaze upon the shredder while their gas tanks filled. Even though his shredded hand was his pitching hand, he had seasons with 26, 20, 29, 27, 25, and 21 victories.

The anchor of the team was first baseman Frank Chance. At six feet and 188 pounds—the size of a small middle infielder today—he was, in his day, an imposing figure. At second base was Johnny Evers, the shortstop was Joe Tinker, and the two detested each other because of a dispute about a taxi fare. On September 13, 1905, in an exhibition game played in Bedford, Indiana, spectators were startled to see a fistfight erupt between Tinker and Evers near second base. The Cubs had dressed for the game at their hotel, and Evers had jumped into a hack and headed for the ballpark, leaving Tinker and others to fend for themselves. This led to the fight, which led, the next day, to them agreeing not to speak to each other. They played together, in sullen silence, for seven more seasons. According to one of baseball's durable myths, they played magically well together, so well that their proficiency at turning double plays became the subject of a famous and god-awful poem, "Baseball's Sad Lexicon," published in the July 18, 1910, edition of the *New York Evening Mail*:

These are the saddest of possible words:
"Tinker to Evers to Chance."
Trio of bear cubs, and fleeter than birds,
"Tinker and Evers and Chance"
Ruthlessly pricking our gonfalon bubble,
Making a Giant hit into a double—
Words that are weighty with nothing but
   trouble:
"Tinker to Evers to Chance."

The poem was written by a reporter with a presidential name, Franklin Pierce Adams, whose editor needed something to fill space. Largely, one suspects, because of this poem, there is space in the Hall of Fame filled, unjustly, by bronze plaques for Tinker and Evers. Their career batting averages, .262 and .270, are rather low for non-pitchers who are in the Hall of Fame without sparkling power-hitting or defensive credentials.

Facts, those stubborn things, prick the bubble of the Tinker-to-Evers-to-Chance fable. In their seasons of greatest Cubs success, 1906–1909, their double play totals were 8, 7, 8, and 6, for a less than grand four-year total of 29 and an average of 7.25 per season. In the 2012 season, the thirty major league teams averaged 142 double plays. The Cubs, while losing 101 games, still "turned two" 148 times.

The 1906 West Side Cubs—or Spuds, as some writers still called them—won 116 games in a 155-game season. From the beginning of August through the end of the season they were an absurd 50 and 8 (with one tie), including winning streaks of 11, 12, and 14 games. The 116 wins are still the major league record, even though the seasons have been 162 games since 1961. The 1954 Cleveland Indians hold the American League record for the most wins in a 154-game season, with 111. The 2001 Seattle Mariners won 116 in a 162-game season. All of which suggest that the 1906 Cubs' .763 winning percentage may be one of baseball's most durable records.

The 1906 American League pennant was won by the White Sox, as the White Stockings were beginning to be called. That year they were also called the "Hitless Wonders," having finished last in their league in hits, home runs, and batting average (.230). Chicago is a city of ethnic enclaves, and the World Series not only pitted the Cubs against the White Sox but the Germans against the Irish. Golenbock says the Germans favored the Cubs, who had players named Schulte, Sheckard, Steinfeldt, Reulbach, Pfiester, Hofman, and Kling. The Irish supported the Sox, with players named Walsh, Donahue, O'Neill, Dougherty, and Sullivan. The White Sox won the Series, 4 games to 2.

In 1907, the Cubs again won the National League pennant, helped by twenty-three wins by a melodiously named pitcher, Orval Overall, from a California town named, of course, Farmersville. The Cubs swept the Detroit Tigers in the World Series. In 1908, they won another pennant and again trounced the Tigers, this time in five games, becoming the first team to win consecutive championships. In

1908, the year "Take Me Out to the Ballgame" was first sung, no one suspected that more than a century would pass without the Cubs winning a third title.

The next season, in a harbinger of things to come, their catcher, Johnny Kling, abandoned baseball to become a professional billiards player. Remarkably, the Cubs won 104 games but finished second, behind the Pirates, who won 110. Soon the Cubs were shedding some expensive players, and players throughout the major leagues were becoming resentful and restless because their salaries were kept low by the lack of negotiating leverage, which was the result of the reserve clause. This gave rise to a rival league, the Federal League, which signed many American League and National League players, including Joe Tinker and Mordecai Brown.

Charles Weeghman, who owned a slew of Chicago lunch restaurants, owned Chicago's Federal League team for the two years, 1914 and 1915, before the league collapsed. His midwestern team, on the shores of Lake Michigan and a long way from salt water, was named, perhaps whimsically, the Whales. It won the 1915 Federal League pennant. Encouraged by the Whales' success and looking to the future, Weeghman had built, on the land purchased from Chicago Theological Lutheran Seminary, a $250,000 ballpark at the corner of Clark and Addison Streets. However, the Federal League had no future and failed after the 1915 season. Before the 1916 season, before the corpse of the Federal League was cold, Weeghman bought an interest in the Cubs and moved them from the West

1915: Horses and horseless carriages.

Side Grounds to Weeghman Park, which seated sixteen thousand.

Weeghman had some interesting friends. One of his partners in his early days as a Cubs owner was oilman Harry F. Sinclair, who had been an organizer of the Federal League. In 1922, Albert B. Fall, the secretary of the interior in the administration of President Warren G. Harding, leased to Mammoth Oil Company, one of Sinclair's subsidiaries, the exclusive right to develop the oil and gas reserves near Casper, Wyoming, beneath a geological formation known as Teapot Dome. The lease was granted without competitive bidding, a fact that seemed suspiciously related to Sinclair's generous contributions to Harding's 1920 campaign. Before the dust settled from the many investigations, both Sinclair and Fall went to prison.

Another of Weeghman's colorful friends was Arnold Rothstein, a New York gambler. He was widely suspected of being the mastermind behind the Black Sox scandal—the fixing of the 1919 World Series, in which the heavily favored White Sox lost to the Cincinnati Reds. In F. Scott Fitzgerald's *The Great Gatsby*, Gatsby and Fitzgerald's narrator, Nick Carraway, are having lunch in a restaurant with a Meyer Wolfsheim, whom Fitzgerald, perhaps reflecting the anti-Semitism of his time, describes as eating "with ferocious delicacy" and wearing cuff links made of what Wolfsheim calls the "finest specimens of human molars." When Wolfsheim leaves the table, Gatsby tells Carraway, "He's the man who fixed the World Series back in 1919." Carraway muses:

> The idea staggered me. I remembered, of course, that the World Series had been fixed in 1919, but if I had thought of it at all I would have thought of it as a thing that merely *happened*, the end of some inevitable chain. It never occurred to me that one man could start to play with the faith of fifty million people—with the single-mindedness of a burglar blowing a safe.

Actually, a remarkable amount about the Black Sox scandal remains speculation, but undoubtedly baseball back then was entangled with unsavory people and practices from the world of gambling. In *Rothstein: The Life, Times and Murder of the Criminal Genius Who Fixed the 1919 World Series*, David Pietrusza makes it clear that Rothstein—certainly Fitzgerald's model for Wolfsheim—

was intimately involved with the shady dealings of Charles Stoneham, a New York financier and gambler and the owner of the New York Giants. Meyer Lansky, a founding father of organized crime in America, was a young associate of Rothstein's. Lansky was the model for Hyman Roth, the gangster who in *The Godfather: Part II* tells Michael Corleone, "I loved baseball ever since Rothstein fixed the World Series in 1919." Such facts are discordant with the narrative of Wrigley Field as a sonnet of sweetness and light. But they underscore this truth: At the time, baseball was a rough business and not as fastidious as it should have been about the company it kept.

This was so even before the front row of the box seats at Wrigley Field was occupied by an unsavory fan from the South Side, Al Capone. When Bill Veeck Jr. was a student at Kenyon College, in Gambier, Ohio, he was summoned home by the news that his father, then president of the Cubs, was ill with incurable leukemia. In his 1962 memoir, *Veeck as in Wreck*, Bill Jr. wrote, "I was determined that he would go out in some comfort and some style," drinking champagne. And Bill knew that the best of this drink could be acquired by someone who had spent happy afternoons in Wrigley Field:

> I hurried to Al Capone's headquarters at the Hotel Metropole and told him what I wanted, and why. "Kid," he said, "I'll send a case of champagne right over." The case was there when I got back. Every morning during these last few days of my

father's life, a case of imported champagne was delivered to the door. The last nourishment that passed between my daddy's lips on this earth was Al Capone's champagne.

When Judge Kenesaw Mountain Landis, the commissioner of baseball, objected to Cubs chatting up Al Capone when he sat in a front row box seat, Gabby Hartnett, a longtime Cub player and manager, supposedly said, "If you don't want me to talk to the big fellow, Judge, why don't you tell him yourself?" This looks like one of those suspiciously perfect quotes that journalists refer to as "too good to check."

Hartnett was what Chicagoans back then called "an old-neighborhood guy," by which they meant he never stopped being approachable. If you invited him to dinner, he was apt to come. It was in response to such a dinner invitation that Hartnett met his future wife. Roberts Ehrgott, in *Mr. Wrigley's Ball Club: Chicago and the Cubs During the Jazz Age*, reports that when Hartnett was invited to a high school prom, he went. The student who invited him had made his acquaintance when Hartnett visited the baseball team's practice at St. Cyril High School, where he knew the football coach. During the practice Hartnett peeled off his jacket and hit some fly balls to the team. One of the adolescents shagging flies was James Farrell, who in the 1930s would publish the Studs Lonigan trilogy: *Young Lonigan, The Young Manhood of Studs Lonigan*, and *Judgment Day*. These deeply depressing novels of ethnic strife, family tensions, and material hardship on Chicago's South Side during the Depression tell the story of a young man struggling, and failing, to cope with life. But the author of these dark stories of naturalism and realism knew how to light up a prom.

Golenbock says that under Weeghman in 1916, the Cubs became the first team to adopt the policy of allowing fans to keep balls batted into the stands. This concern for improving the fans' ballpark experience would become the defining aspect of the Cubs' ownership under another Chicago businessman who in 1916 also bought a portion of the team's shares. He was a chewing-gum magnate named William Wrigley.

Wrigley arrived in Chicago with his net worth—thirty-two dollars—in his wallet and lived to build the Wrigley Building, the first major office building north of the Chicago River, at the southern end of what now is known as Michigan Avenue's Magnificent Mile. In every fiber of his being, Wrigley was a promoter. Wrigley's father made soap, which William was on the road selling, from a wagon drawn by a four-horse team with jangling bells on its harness, as he said, "before I was thirteen." He gave purchasers of his soap samples of free baking soda—until there was more demand for the baking soda than for the soap. Then he began selling the baking soda and giving customers free chewing gum—until demand for the chewing gum became so strong that Wrigley decided to manufacture and sell it. And to promote it with expensive advertising campaigns.

Wrigley was excessively fond of saying, "Baseball is too much of a sport to be a business and too much of a business to be a sport." To be sure, the Supreme Court, in a dotty opinion written in 1922 by Oliver Wendell Holmes, had secured Major League Baseball's exemption from antitrust regulation by declaring that baseball is not a business engaged in interstate commerce. But as the late Jim Murray, a sports columnist for the *Los Angeles Times*, said, "If baseball is not a business, then General Motors is a sport." Baseball has always been a business, and one that punishes owners who treat it instead as a hobby.

In the 1920s, when Chicago's population grew 25 percent, two-thirds of the city's residents had been born abroad or were the children of parents who had been. For this polyglot city with so many newcomers, baseball—rooting for the home team in your new hometown—was part of the Americanization process. Learning to talk baseball was part of the catechism of the civic religion. In Chicago, the language of baseball could be learned by listening to the radio.

Today, when the word "connectivity" describes life in a world in which everything is instantly available to everyone everywhere on portable devices, it is impossible to recapture the magic of radio in the 1920s, when a hotel could claim to be truly posh if it provided a radio in every room. For rural Americans, radio ameliorated the loneliness of empty spaces. For urban Americans, many of whom were not long separated from rural roots, radio assuaged another kind of loneliness: the anonymity of crowds. Listeners to particular programs became members of consumption communities, which were electronic neighborhoods of shared experiences, information, and diversions. This was particularly so for urban women tending to households before the postwar influx of women into the workforce during and after the Second World War.

The first radio broadcast of a major league game was produced by Pittsburgh's KDKA in 1921 during the Pirates pennant race with the Giants. In Cincinnati, a radio station broadcast the first game of the 1924 season. Radio stations were multiplying rapidly, from 382 in 1922 to 681 in 1927. The number of radios in use in America rose from 60,000 in 1922 to 1.5 million in 1923 to 3 million in 1924 to 16.6 million in 1932. Stations were ravenous for content, and Chicago stations had, in William Wrigley, a businessman with hundreds of hours of content he was eager to supply without charge.

When Wrigley decided to give away Cubs baseball to Chicago radio stations, the stations decided the price was right. "By mid-1929," Ehrgott writes, "most major Chicago stations had made Cub home games their staple, effectively eliminating afternoon alternatives from Chicago airwaves seventy-seven afternoons a year." The fact that the stations were not interested in paying the costs of broadcasting away games indicates that they were more attracted by free content than they were convinced that a large audience was eager for baseball. But the audience was growing, and not just in the city. One farmer within range of a Chicago station wrote a thank-you note to the Cubs: "Don't stop it. I have a radio in the field with me. I plow one turn, sit down for a cool drink out of the jug and listen to the score. It's grand."

The 1920s also saw the birth of ballyhoo and the manufacturing of celebrity. This was a result of the interrelated burgeoning of radio, tabloid journalism, advertising, public relations, and sports superstars like Babe Ruth, Jack Dempsey, Red Grange, Bill Tilden, and Man o' War. The age of celebrity was both cause and effect of the most socially transformative technologies of the 1920s: radio and cinema. About radio, William Wrigley was ahead of his time. Most baseball owners saw radio as a threat, fearing that it would cause people to follow the team from the comfort of their couches rather than the grandstands of the home field. Wrigley the chewing-gum marketer saw radio as a way to whet fans' appetites for a day at the ballpark. His policy about broadcasts was: The more the merrier. At one point, five different stations were carrying home games. One of the play-by-play announcers was a very young Russ Hodges. The career he started in Wrigley Field would have its most memorable moment in New York's Polo Grounds on October 3, 1951, when he was working for the Giants. Bobby Thomson's pennant-winning home run—"the shot heard 'round the world"—elicited from him the most famous home-run call in baseball history: "The Giants win the pennant! The Giants win the pennant! The Giants win the pennant!"

In 1927, the year Ruth electrified the nation by hitting sixty home runs in American League ballparks, the Cubs became the first National League team to pull more than a million fans into their park. In the 1920s, Americans generally, and Chicagoans especially, had an insatiable appetite for sports. This was dramatized on the city's lakefront in 1927 when more—many more, according to some reports—than one hundred thousand spectators poured into Soldier Field, then just three years old, for the heavyweight fight between champion Gene Tunney and former champion Jack Dempsey. Not all those at ringside with Al Capone were locals. Among the luminaries who were there to see, or be seen, were Bernard Baruch, Charlie Chaplin, Douglas Fairbanks, Gloria Swanson, Princess Xenia of Russia, and American royalty in the form of captains of industry.

Between 1925 and 1929, when many stations were broadcasting Cubs home games, Cubs attendance surged 140 percent. In 1929, the year in which the stock market crashed, fifteen days after the Philadelphia Athletics beat the Cubs in the fifth and final game of the World Series, the Cubs' home attendance was 1,485,166. This was more than any major league team would draw until the Depression and the Second World War were over, more than the Cubs would draw while winning the 1945 pennant (1,036,386), and more than they would draw until the almost-magic year of 1969 (1,674,993).

In the 1929 Labor Day doubleheader, a morning and then an afternoon game, with the Cubs charging separate admissions, an estimated 81,000 fans packed Wrigley

Field, probably the largest number of fans to visit a ballpark on a single day until 82,871 flocked to Cleveland Municipal Stadium—"the Mistake on the Lake"—for an Indians-Athletics doubleheader on June 20, 1948. On April 9, 1993, the Colorado Rockies, an expansion team, drew 80,227 to its first home game, which was played in Mile High Stadium, then the home of the NFL Denver Broncos. All of which was almost equal to the St. Louis Browns' home attendance for the entire 1935 season: 80,922.

For the 1929 World Series, the Cubs' management enlarged Wrigley's seating capacity by adding 8,000 bleacher seats, looming halfway across Waveland and Sheffield Avenues. The Cubs also packed Wrigley Field by putting spectators *on* the field. Ehrgott reports that during the 1920s, "one of every four National League customers passed through Mr. Wrigley's turnstiles." And this was before Mr. Wrigley's ballpark had a second deck. The right-field bleachers were "a country fair–style structure of scaffolding and planks whose first row met the playing field behind a cyclone fence only 320 feet from home plate." On weekends, up to 4,000 customers—as many as some major league teams were putting in their seats on normal days—watched the Cubs not from the seats, which were full, but standing on the outfield grass, behind ropes held by the Andy Frain ushers, resplendent in their blue-and-gold uniforms.

One benefit for these standing-room spectators was that they could chat with the outfielders. And they could give the Cubs a home field advantage: When the visiting team hit a long fly ball, the fans would move back, pulling the rope with them, thereby expanding the field of play for the benefit of the Cubs' outfielders. And when the Cubs hit a fly ball close to the rope line, the crowd would surge forward a few feet, turning a probable out into a home run.

One of William Wrigley's better ideas—it illustrated his flair for promoting his products—was to give away admission to Wrigley Field to hundreds of thousands of people every year. The idea was Ladies' Day, announced in newspaper advertisements like this one:

LADIES' DAY

Mothers
Daughters
Sisters
Wives
Grandmothers

You are again to be the invited guests of the Chicago National League Ball Club.

It's official Ladies' Day at the prettiest baseball grounds in the world.

ADMISSION FREE

The number of women who were admitted free in the 1920s and early 1930s probably did, as Ehrgott says, exceed some teams' *paid* attendance each season. In 1930, the twelve Ladies' Days drew 240,000 women, many dressed to the nines in hats and fine frocks. Those who had to stand behind ropes in the outfield, the grandstand being full to overflowing, could feel their heels sinking into the turf. That year, the St. Louis Browns' season attendance was 152,088; the Pirates drew 357,795; and the Reds, 386,727.

"I spend $1.5 million a year for advertising," Wrigley explained. "I manufacture chewing gum and give samples away to the public. I own a ball club in the National League and I give away samples of baseball." Recipients of free samples developed a taste for both products. The Cubs estimated that on Sundays, when the team drew its largest crowds and women paid, like everyone else, 35 percent of the fans were female.

On Friday, June 27, 1929, approximately 30,000 women showed up for free admission, leaving room for only about 15,000 paying customers. After that, the Cubs limited Ladies' Day tickets to 17,500.

But the Cubs still ran ads in the *Tribune* saying, "The Chicago National League Club wants every woman to acquaint herself with the joys and thrills of baseball." Some ads offered reassurance to the timid: "You don't need an escort."

There were, however, occasions when people needed

protection from the ladies, who could be disorderly in their rush for admission to the ballpark and for choice seats. Wrigley, who said, "It is easier to control a crowd of 100,000 men than of 10,000 women," told this story: "One Friday, shortly after the gates were open, and there were 45,000 spectators inside and thousands outside, an usher came upon a little old woman who was crying. He assured her that he would find her a seat somewhere. 'I don't want a seat,' she sobbed. 'I want to get out. I came to visit my daughter, who lives near here. Before I knew it I was caught in this terrible mob and swept inside.'"

Which is why a Chicago newspaper ran the following doggerel:

> I saw a wounded baseball fan tottering down
>   the street,
> Encased in bandages and tape, and bruised
>   from head to feet;
> And as I called the ambulance, I heard
>   the poor guy say:
> "I bought a seat in Wrigley Field, but it was
>   ladies' day."

In July 1926, the *Chicago Tribune* carried this little item:

WHIPPED FOR STAYING OUT LATE, GIRL RUNS AWAY

Violet Popovich, 15 years old, 4516 E. Harrison Street, was whipped for going to a movie with a boy and staying out late last Sunday night. Monday she ran away from home and yesterday the Fillmore Street police were asked to find her.

Violet ran away from home—such as it may have been; she spent much of her childhood in an orphanage—at age fifteen. At seventeen, when she started calling herself Violet Valli, she became a dancer in a chorus line. At eighteen, she married. And along the way she became rather too interested in the Cubs. Or at least some of them. And some ballplayers who were not Cubs. Ehrgott found that a Chicago paper had reported that before she met Billy Jurges, Valli had been "friendly" with at least one other major league player, one with a Cubs uniform in his future: Leo Durocher, then a Cincinnati Reds infielder.

When Abraham Lincoln met Harriet Beecher Stowe, the author of *Uncle Tom's Cabin*, the novel that added fuel to the slavery controversy, he supposedly (this comes from Stowe family lore) addressed her as "the little lady who started the big war." Violet Valli was the spark that lit

Leo Durocher: Nice guys need not apply.

the fuse that led to the most famous event in the history of Wrigley Field, an event that almost certainly did not happen.

Not that that matters. The fact is that most baseball fans believe that Babe Ruth actually hit a "called shot" during the 1932 World Series. So it is part of the ballpark's story, even though no one will ever really know whether Ruth

Ruth hits the "called shot." Or not.

pointed to designate the spot in the center-field bleachers where, a moment later, he hit the pitch thrown by the
Cubs' Charlie Root.

A good tutor about this episode is Leigh Montville,
who, in his 2006 biography, *The Big Bam: The Life and
Times of Babe Ruth*, begins the story with "Violet (What I
Did for Love) Valli—the Most Talked About Woman in
Chicago." That is how she was billed during her scheduled
twenty-two-week vaudeville show. In 1932, she was twenty-
one and smitten with Billy Jurges, twenty-four, the Cubs'
shortstop. His affections may once, or occasionally, have
been as ardent for her as hers were for him, but his were
decidedly less constant.

So on July 6, 1932, Violet, packing a .25-caliber revolver, went to the room at the Hotel Carlos where Jurges

lived during the season. Having written a farewell note telling her brother that "life without Billy isn't worth living," she intended to kill Billy and then herself. Jurges admitted her to his room, and when she began to execute her plan, he disarmed her, but not before taking two bullets: one in the ribs, the other in a hand. He and she, together for one last time, were rushed to the same hospital.

The judge presiding over a dispute about possession of some inconvenient letters between Valli and Jurges—and perhaps another Cubs star—made clear his judicial priorities: "I want to keep this case under my jurisdiction to prevent embarrassment to the Cubs so that their chances of winning the pennant will not be harmed. I don't want this thing to worry Jurges."

The Cubs had another worry: They needed a shortstop without a bullet wound. So they signed Mark Koenig. He had played that position five years earlier on what many people consider the best team in baseball history, the 1927 Yankees. He had hit a triple and scored when Ruth hit his sixtieth home run. Koenig had been released by the Tigers in the spring of 1932 and was playing for the San Francisco Seals when the Cubs called. He promptly joined the team, and his .353 batting average for the Cubs helped them win the pennant by four games over the Pirates.

But before the World Series began, the Cubs' players voted on the distribution of the team's World Series payout and awarded Koenig only a half share. The winner's share of the 1932 World Series would turn out to be $5,231.77, and each of the losers would get $4,244.60. Koenig's former teammates on the Yankees were not amused, and they expressed their (somewhat opportunistic) indignation in what used to be called "bench jockeying." Ruth, exuberant in most things, was especially so in excoriating the Cubs as cheapskates. Ruth did this even though there was no love lost between him and Koenig; Ruth had grappled with the shortstop in a clubhouse fight when Koenig made a disparaging remark about Ruth's new wife, Claire.

The Cubs, Montville writes, responded to the Yankees' insults "with questions about [Ruth's] parentage, his increasing weight, his racial features, his sexual preferences, and whatever else they could invent." In the rough-and-tumble world of baseball back then, the word "nigger" was bandied about casually. "It was," says Montville correctly, "all familiar baseball stuff for the time, but with an exaggerated edge."

The Yankees won the first two games, in New York, and arrived at Wrigley Field for Game 3 to see a strong wind blowing out toward right field. In the top of the first inning, with two runners on, and after two lemons had been thrown at him from the stands, Ruth homered off Charlie Root. In the third, Ruth flied out to deep right center. In the fifth, with the score 4–4, the bases empty, and Root still on the mound, Ruth took a first pitch for a called strike. Then, Montville writes, Ruth looked toward the Cubs' dugout and "put up one finger, as if to say, 'That's just one strike.'" Ruth might have been responding to a Cubs pitcher, Guy Bush, who was standing on the top step of the dugout. After Root threw two pitches that were called balls, Ruth took a second called strike and this time held up two fingers. "He then pointed," says Montville. "Where he pointed is a question, but legend has it that he pointed to dead center field." What we do know, and perhaps all that we know for sure, is this from Montville:

> Cubs catcher Gabby Hartnett later said that Ruth said, "It only takes one to hit." [Lou] Gehrig, in the on-deck circle, said Ruth said to Root, "I'm going to knock the next one down your god-damned throat." A pair of 16mm home movies discovered more than half a century later seemed to indicate that Ruth might have pointed at the Cubs bench and at Bush rather than dead center field (maybe Ruth wanted to knock the ball down Bush's goddamned throat?), but both films were taken from angles that left room for doubt.

Be that as it may, Ruth hit Root's next pitch, a slow curve, up into the wind and out of the park between the center-field scoreboard and the right-field bleachers. Montville says that as Ruth rounded third in front of the Cubs' dugout, he held up four fingers: Four bases? Four games? Gehrig knocked Root's next pitch out of the park, and the Yankees won Game 3, 7–5. The next day they completed their sweep, 13–6.

Only one reporter among the throng of newspaperman at the game said in his story that before Root delivered the pitch, Ruth pointed to where he was going to hit it. But the Scripps Howard News Service, for which Joe Williams wrote, headlined his story "Ruth Calls Shot." So there.

The truth is that the truth will never be known. But as Montville says, Ruth had a showman's boisterous habit of promising to hit home runs for this or that person or occasion, and often did. On some later occasions, Ruth claimed that he called his shot in Game 3 of the Series. On other occasions, he said that "only a damn fool" would do such a thing. The next spring, however, he attended a New York cocktail party hosted by the most famous sportswriter of the day, Grantland Rice. There the wife of the most famous political columnist of the day, Walter Lippmann, asked Ruth what had happened the previous autumn. In his 1955 autobiography, *The Tumult and the Shouting*, Rice recounted Ruth's response, but without Ruth's tangy language, which Montville supplies for our less decorous age:

> "The Cubs had fucked my old teammate Mark Koenig by cutting him for only a measly fucken half share of the Series money. Well, I'm riding the fuck out of the Cubs, telling 'em they're the cheapest pack of fucken crumbums in the world. . . . [Root] breezes the first two pitches by—both strikes! The mob's tearing down Wrigley Field. I shake my fist after that first strike. After the second I point my bat at these bellerin' bleachers— right where I aim to park the ball. Root throws it and I hit that fucken ball on the nose, right over the fence for two fucken runs. 'How do you like

those apples, you fucken bastard?' I yell at Root
as I run toward first. By the time I reach home
I'm almost fallin' down I'm laughing so fucken
hard—and that's how it happened."

Montville notes that Ruth's memory was not perfect:
The count was 2–2, not 0–2, and there was no one on base.
Mrs. Lippmann and her spouse quickly left the party, and
Rice asked Ruth, "Why'd you use that language?" Ruth re-
plied, "You heard her ask me what happened. So I told her."

Montville offers a further bit of evidence that *something*
special happened in Game 3 to make the Cubs irritable.
Guy Bush was the Cubs' starting pitcher in Game 4. When
Ruth came to the plate in the first inning—even though
there were runners on first and second and no one out and
the Cubs were facing elimination from the Series—Bush
used his first pitch, a fastball, to hit Ruth. But if, the day
before, Ruth had pointed to center field after the second
pitch from Root in the fifth inning, the third pitch probably would have come at his head. Really.

Take a long look at the hard glare coming at you from
the photograph on page 62. Does that seem like the sort
of fellow who would have tolerated disrespectful behavior
from anyone, even Babe Ruth? Charlie Root was a pitcher
who, a Brooklyn baseball writer said, seemed to throw
at Dodger hitters "for the sheer fun of it." Because Root
seemed to go through life with his chin jutting in defiance,
Cubs manager Charlie Grimm nicknamed him Chinski.
Root was so thoroughly not amused by the whole "called

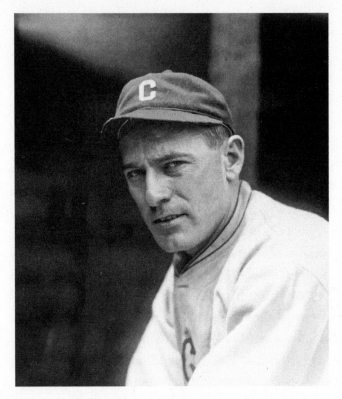

Charlie Root: Would Babe Ruth provoke him?

shot" story that he turned down an offer to play himself in the movie *The Babe Ruth Story.*

Root's accomplishments during sixteen seasons with the Cubs rank him as the fourth-best pitcher in the team's history, behind only Mordecai Brown, Grover Cleveland Alexander, and Ferguson Jenkins. Root holds the team record for career wins (201) and innings pitched (3,137.1). Yet he is remembered only for one pitch.

One fan at this memorable game was a twelve-year-old named John Paul Stevens who would grow up to serve thirty-five years as a justice on the U.S. Supreme Court. At age ninety-three, in 2013, he was still a Cub fan and still convinced that Ruth did indeed point to a spot in the bleachers and hit a ball there. Stevens was also cheerfully resigned to the fact that he might be more often remembered for having been at Wrigley that day than for having been on the court all those years.

Seated along the first-base line on this myth-making day, behind the Yankees' dugout, was the governor of New York, Franklin Delano Roosevelt, who then was thirty-eight days from being elected president. FDR made the ceremonial first pitch from among the box seats. At his side was his host, Chicago's Democratic mayor, Anton J. Cermak, the city's only foreign-born mayor. The two were a study in contrasts.

While FDR was a Hudson Valley patrician, Cermak had been born in 1873 in Bohemia in the Austro-Hungarian Empire, about twenty miles from Prague. The day he turned one year old, he was on Ellis Island. His family found its way to Illinois, where, as a boy, he worked in coal mines near Joliet. When he was sixteen, he moved to Chicago and rose through the ranks of the city's Democratic machine, earning the nickname "Tough Tony" and throwing large picnics for supporters, at which he illegally sold one-dollar mugs of beer from one hundred barrels donated by a North Side bootlegger. He was elected mayor in 1931. Cermak had opposed the nomination of FDR, preferring the candidacy of another up-from-nothing ethnic politician, New York's former governor and FDR rival, Al Smith, the party's 1928 nominee. Cermak would, however, again be with FDR 137 days after witnessing Ruth's home run.

At about nine-thirty P.M. on February 15, 1933, in Miami, Florida, FDR, now the president-elect, stepped off a yacht on which he had been fishing in the Bahamas. He delivered a short speech to onlookers, among whom was Cermak, who was in Miami to talk patronage with James A. Farley, chairman of the Democratic National Committee. Then FDR gestured for Cermak to join him at his open touring car. Also in the crowd was another immigrant, Giuseppe Zangara from Italy, who had a boiling hatred of politicians. He was only five feet, one inch tall, but he stood on a bench, drew an eight-dollar pistol, and fired five shots toward the car. A woman in the crowd hit his gun hand and the crowd overwhelmed him, but not before his bullets struck Cermak and three other bystanders.

The assumption is that Zangara's target was Roosevelt, and there is no contrary evidence. Chicago being Chicago, however, there are rival theories. One turns on the fact that on December 19, 1932, the mayor sent two detectives to the office of Frank Nitti, who had become ascendant in Chicago crime when Al Capone was sent to prison on charges of tax evasion. Nitti had no gun but was shot three times by the detectives, one of whom supposedly shot his own hand and then claimed that Nitti shot him and the detectives fired back in self-defense. Nitti survived. Cermak headed for Florida.

Cermak died on March 6. Just fourteen days after that—the wheels of Florida justice did not grind slowly—Zangara was electrocuted.

As Cermak was rushed to the hospital in FDR's car, he supposedly said, "I'm glad it was me and not you." Isn't it pretty to think so. Cermak's noble words, which are about as plausible as Ruth's called shot, are on a plaque in Miami's Bayfront Park, where the shooting occurred, and are carved on the wall of the marble mausoleum in which Cermak is buried, in Chicago's Bohemian National Cemetery, about five miles from Wrigley Field.

What became of Violet Valli? For a while, in a theater near the Loop, she starred as "the Girl Who Shot for Love" in a show called "Bare Cub Follies."

Before we leave the subject of Game 3 of the 1932 World Series, it should be mentioned that this was not the only time an aggrieved and armed woman had consequences at Wrigley Field.

The headline on the obituary in the *New York Times* of March 24, 2013, read, "Ruth Ann Steinhagen Is Dead at 83; Shot a Ballplayer." She had actually died the previous December 29, but no public attention was paid until a staffer at the *Chicago Tribune*, while researching an unrelated article, stumbled upon a notice of her death.

Hers was a story of the peculiar melancholy of madness.

Born in the South Side suburb of Cicero, by the time she graduated from a Chicago high school she had a pattern of falling in love with famous men from a distance. Her fixations included the movie star Alan Ladd and the Cubs' outfielder Peanuts Lowrey. Her interest in Eddie Waitkus, the Cubs' first baseman, became an obsession. Because he was the son of Lithuanian immigrants, she studied the Lithuanian language and listened to Lithuanian radio broadcasts. Because he was from near Boston—he graduated from high school in Cambridge and attended Boston College—she began craving baked beans. With a calm lucidity unique to a lunatic, she said, in a court-ordered autobiographical essay, "As time went on, I just became nuttier and nuttier about the guy."

When the Cubs traded Waitkus to the Phillies following the 1948 season, Steinhagen suffered a breakdown. Although she held a job as a typist for an insurance company, she moved into a small apartment less than three miles from Wrigley Field, and in this apartment she built a shrine to Waitkus that included scorecards, newspaper clippings, photographs, and fifty ticket stubs. And there she decided to kill the object of her veneration.

When the Phillies came to Chicago in June 1949, she took a room at the Edgewater Beach Hotel, where the team stayed, and paid a bellhop five dollars to deliver a note inviting Waitkus to her room. Having fortified herself with two whiskey sours and a daiquiri, she admitted him to her room around eleven-thirty P.M. "For two years, you've been bothering me and now you're going to die," she told him. Waitkus, who had survived two years with the army in the Pacific during the Second World War, and who had won four bronze stars, might have died if Steinhagen had fired a weapon more powerful than a .22-caliber rifle. She called the hotel's front desk, said she had shot a man, and waited by Waitkus's side until the police arrived.

He was back with the Phillies later that year. In 1950, he hit .284 for the pennant-winning "Whiz Kids" and was named Comeback Player of the Year. In 1952, the novelist Bernard Malamud, who was not a baseball fan but knew a good story when he saw one, and who perhaps had noticed that early in Waitkus's career sportswriters had referred to him as a "natural," published *The Natural*, the story of Roy Hobbs, who is shot by a woman.

Three weeks after the 1949 shooting, a judge declared Steinhagen insane, and she was institutionalized in Kankakee State Hospital, where she underwent electroconvulsive therapy to alter the chemistry of her brain. Released after three years, she lived in quiet anonymity until her death at home on the Northwest Side. Waitkus had died in 1972, at age fifty-three.

The most remarkable Cubs career of Wrigley Field's prewar years made up with gaudy numbers what it lacked in longevity. Like the country itself, Lewis Robert "Hack" Wilson's career roared in the intoxicating, and intoxicated, 1920s. And like the country, it crashed spectacularly in the 1930s. He was born with the twentieth century but would not live to see its second half. Yet one record he set will probably survive into the twenty-second.

It is not certain how Wilson came to be called Hack. Some say it was because his first major league manager, John McGraw, thought he resembled a taxicab, which back then was commonly called a hack. Others say it was because he brought to mind Cubs outfielder Hack Miller, supposedly the strongest man in baseball. The most common and plausible explanation, however, is that Wilson looked like a popular wrestler and strong man of the day, George Hackenschmidt. Whatever the derivation of Wilson's nickname, he was one of baseball's stranger sights.

He stood five feet, six inches and weighed at least 190 pounds even when in tip-top shape, which he rarely achieved because he never was a martyr to the strictures of sensible living. He had an eighteen-inch neck, an ample belly, and wore size 5½ or 6 shoes. He has been described as a mixture of "suet and swat." He was a human fireplug whom Arthur Daley described as built like "two men sitting down." Another sportswriter said Wilson resembled a beer keg, the contents of which Wilson was all too familiar with. His flat face is a characteristic correlated with fetal alcohol syndrome. So is a problem with impulse control.

He was born on April 26, 1900, in Ellwood City, Pennsylvania, a town of hard men doing hard work in steel mills and locomotive works about forty miles north of Pittsburgh. His mother, who never married his father, was sixteen when he was born. Both parents drank too much, and his mother died of appendicitis at age twenty-four, when her son was seven. He left school in the sixth grade to toil as a printer's apprentice and ironworker until, in 1921, the lure of baseball brought him to Martinsburg, West Virginia, in the Blue Ridge League. By 1923, he was with John McGraw's New York Giants. McGraw, a martinet, was not amused by Wilson's fast living off the field, and when Wilson struggled on the field in 1925, the Giants sent him down to the Toledo Mud Hens. For some reason—McGraw blamed a clerical error—the Giants did not renew their option on Wilson, and the Cubs acquired him on waivers for $5,000. He and the toddling town took to each other.

In his second month playing there, on May 24, 1926, wielding the forty-ounce bat he called "Big Bertha," he hit one of the longest home runs in Wrigley Field history to that point. That night he was arrested while trying to escape through a rear window when police raided a saloon that thought, as much of Chicago did, that Prohibition was optional. In 1928, he ignited a Wrigley Field riot when fans poured onto the field after he plunged into the stands to attack a heckler. In 1929, he ran into the visiting team's dugout to punch a Cincinnati Reds pitcher. At Union Station that evening, as the Cubs and Reds were boarding separate trains to different cities, Wilson got into a fight with another Reds player.

An often-told story, probably too good to be true, but certainly too delightful not to tell again, is that Joe McCarthy, the Cubs' manager from 1926 through 1930, tried to scare Wilson into sobriety, or at least moderation. McCarthy filled one glass with water and another with whiskey and dropped a worm into each. The worm in the water moved around without noticeable ill effects; the one in the whiskey promptly died. "So," said McCarthy to Wilson, "what does that teach you?" Wilson replied, "If you drink whiskey, you'll never get worms."

Wilson said, "I never played drunk. Hungover, yes, but never drunk." But Bill Veeck remembered one instance when Cubs trainer Andy Lotshaw had to resort to heroic measures to get Wilson ready to go out to center field:

> Andy had Hack in one of those big, high old tubs, sobering him up. In the tub with Hack was a 50-pound cake of ice. Well, what would you do if a 50-pound cake of ice jumped into your tub with you? You'd try to jump out, right? That was precisely what Hack was trying to do. Enthusiastically but not successfully. Every time Hack's head would bob up, Andy would shove it back down under the water and the cake of ice would come bobbing up. It was a fascinating sight, watching them bob in perfect rhythm, first Hack's head, then the ice, then Hack's head, then the ice.

That afternoon, Wilson hit three home runs. Some baseball executive might have been tempted to say something like what Abraham Lincoln said about General Ulysses S. Grant's drinking: Find out what he drinks and send some of it to my other generals. In 1926, Wilson batted .321, drove in 109 runs, and hit 21 home runs, which may not seem very impressive by today's standards but was good enough to lead the National League. The next year he tied for the league home-run lead with 30, and in 1928 his 31 again tied for the league lead. In 1929, Wilson batted .345 with a league-leading 159 RBIs and the Cubs won their first pennant since 1918. The Cubs lost the World Series to Connie Mack's Philadelphia Athletics, partly because in Game 4, with the Cubs leading 8–0, the Athletics scored 10 runs in the seventh inning when Wilson lost two fly balls in the sun. After the game, when a boy asked Cubs manager Joe McCarthy for a ball, McCarthy supposedly replied, "Come back tomorrow and stand behind Wilson and you'll be able to pick up all the balls you want." The following year would be better.

It is unclear why baseball went haywire in 1930. That it did so is written in numbers that are, strictly speaking, incredible. They are to be believed because the events they recorded really happened. They are, however, to be disbelieved because they are so aberrant, so discontinuous with seasons before and since, that they must be taken as evidence that for one year something was done to the ball. Some say it was wound differently—tighter, presumably. Others say, mysteriously, that it was wound with yarn made from Australian wool, although it is unclear why that wool would have made such a difference. Never mind. These are the indisputable facts:

The National League—yes, *the league*—hit .303, and thirty-three National League players hit .300 or better. Three American League teams and twenty-nine American League players hit .300 or better. Although the Phillies' Chuck Klein hit .386, he lost the National League batting crown by 15 points to the Giants' Bill Terry, who hit .401. The Cardinals had more than ten .300 hitters. Six major leaguers drove in more than 150 runs each, and thirty-two had 100 or more. The offensive pyrotechnics were on display at Wrigley Field on May 12, 1930, when the Cubs scored 12 unanswered runs and still lost to the Giants, who'd had a 14–0 lead before the Cubs scored their first run, in the fifth inning. Guy Bush had these mind-bending numbers for the season: He allowed 291 hits and 86 walks—377 base runners, not counting hit batters—in 225 innings and had an ugly 6.20 ERA, yet his won-lost record was a respectable 15–10.

Pitchers that season worried about their physical safety as well as their professional standing, and this only made the onslaught worse. Joe Tinker, the retired Cub shortstop, said pitchers were afraid to throw as hard as they could because their follow-throughs might leave them exposed to line drives; Giants manager John McGraw suggested moving the pitcher's mound closer to the plate to give pitchers an advantage. Even Yankee owner Jake Ruppert—whose star player, Babe Ruth, had ignited the craze for long balls and big innings—wanted to see the spitball, which had been banned in 1920, made legal again in order to tame the surge of offense.

No one seems to know what was done to the ball, when it was done, or at whose behest it was done. A livelier ball may have been introduced during the 1929 season; such a ball clearly was in use in 1930. And by 1931, the owners recoiled from the wretched excess of the previous year.

From 1926 through 1930, Hack Wilson batted in 708 runs in 738 games, an average of 141.6 a year. Only Lou Gehrig, Babe Ruth, and Jimmy Foxx have matched or exceeded Wilson's 708 over five seasons.

Wilson's 1930 rampage started fast and then accelerated. In August, he hit 13 home runs and drove in a stupendous total of 53 runs. On September 15, he drove in his 176th run, breaking Lou Gehrig's season record set in 1927, the year Gehrig's teammate Babe Ruth hit 60 home runs. Wilson finished with 56 home runs, a National League record that would stand until 1998, when two pharmacologically assisted sluggers, the Cardinals' Mark McGwire and the Cubs' Sammy Sosa, hit 70 and 66, respectively. McGwire would hit 65 in 1999; Sosa would hit 63 in 1999 and 64 in 2001. But leaving aside these empty tributes to better numbers through chemistry, Wilson's record of 56—itself a product of a somehow-enhanced ball—stood until the Diamondbacks' Luis Gonzalez hit 57 in 2001.

Wilson's major league record of 191 RBIs was challenged the next year when Gehrig drove in 184. In 1937, the Tigers' Hank Greenberg drove in 183. Since the

Second World War, the highest RBI totals in either league by players not suspected of cheating with steroids, human growth hormone, or some other substance are 159 by the Red Sox's Vern Stephens and Ted Williams in 1949, 155 by the Yankees' Joe DiMaggio in 1948, and 153 by the Dodgers' Tommy Davis in 1962.

Bill James, baseball's Newton, who has done as much as anyone to teach baseball how to see itself from new perspectives, believes that Wilson's RBI record has become more secure as team lineups have become more laced with power hitters. In Wilson's day, most teams had few home-run hitters, and they could feast on the RBI opportunities provided by singles hitters getting on base ahead of them. "In modern baseball," James writes in his *Historical Baseball Abstract*, "*everybody* tries to hit home runs, spreading the offense top to bottom, but creating no 'clusters' of RBI opportunities." Which is to say, extreme RBI totals have declined as baseball has become better, with more power distributed throughout batting orders.

From his pinnacle in 1930, Wilson plunged with stunning swiftness. The Cubs changed managers for 1931, replacing Joe McCarthy, who had considerable tolerance for the off-field behavior that accompanied Wilson's on-field accomplishments, with Rogers Hornsby, who, to put it politely, did not specialize in positive reinforcement. The greatest right-handed hitter of all time, Hornsby was such a focused fanatic about being in peak condition to play that he avoided movies, lest they strain his eyes. He was a relentless critic of Wilson, who did not take this well. But

Hack Wilson: "suet and swat."

neither the managerial change nor whatever was done to restore the ball to its pre-1930 condition explains Wilson's downward spiral. His 1931 salary of $33,000 was the National League's highest, but as often happens in baseball, the Cubs were paying for the past, not the present—and certainly not the future. Recalling the winter of 1930, Wilson said, "I spent most of that off-season in tap rooms." He reported to spring training twenty pounds overweight. In 1931, he hit 13 home runs, a decline of 43 home runs from the previous season—a collapse without equal in baseball history. On September 6 of that year, he was suspended without pay for the remainder of the season following a fistfight with reporters on a train in Cincinnati. That winter he was traded to the Cardinals, for whom he never played an inning; they traded him to the Dodgers, for whom he had a productive season (23 home runs and 123 RBIs). But his decline was apparent, and in the middle of the 1934 season, the Dodgers released him. He signed with the Phillies, for whom he had twenty at bats before being released. Less than four seasons after his spectacular 1930, he was out of Major League Baseball. After a season with the Single-A Albany Senators of the New York–Pennsylvania League, he retired. He was thirty-five.

On August 16, 1948, Babe Ruth died. More than one hundred thousand mourners filed past his casket as it lay in Yankee Stadium, and an estimated seventy-five thousand jammed Fifth Avenue outside St. Patrick's Cathedral, where his funeral mass was performed. On November 23, 1948, Hack Wilson died, in Baltimore. He had moderated his drinking, but too late. He died destitute. His body was unclaimed for three days. Ford Frick, the president of the National League, wired $350 to pay for Wilson's funeral. The mortician donated a gray suit for Wilson's body. Shortly before his death, Wilson had given an interview to CBS Radio. This was part of it:

> Talent isn't enough. You need common sense and good advice. If anyone tries to tell you different, tell them the story of Hack Wilson. . . . Kids in and out of baseball who think because they have talent they have the world by the tail. It isn't so. Kids, don't be too big to accept advice. Don't let what happened to me happen to you.

In 1949, a new Cubs manager, Charlie Grimm, who had been Hack Wilson's teammate, framed that portion of Wilson's last interview and hung it in the Cubs' Wrigley Field clubhouse, where it remained for many years.

One Cub's career conformed to the sentimentality that surrounds Wrigley Field because he was practically a boy from the neighborhood. He is also the answer to a nifty trivia question: Who is the only player who was in the major leagues when Babe Ruth hit his last home run, in 1935, and when Henry Aaron hit his first, in 1954? Phil Cavarretta. He graduated in 1934 from Lane Technical High School, which then was 4.7 miles from Wrigley Field. At Lane, as he would with the Cubs, he played first base and outfield, but he also pitched eight one-hitters, and his final game was a no-hitter. He signed with the Cubs before he graduated, at seventeen. The Cubs then sent him to their Peoria farm club, where he slugged a home run in his first at bat as a professional, in a game in which he hit for the cycle. He was eighteen when, on September 16, he joined the Cubs in Brooklyn. On September 25, he hit a home run in his first Wrigley Field at bat to win a 1–0 game. He played in the Cubs' last three World Series: 1935, 1938, and 1945, the year he was named the National League's most valuable player. He played for the Cubs for twenty years, a team record, and was a player-manager in the last three, beginning in 1951.

On March 29, 1954, at a spring training meeting with Philip K. Wrigley, Cavarretta annoyed his employer by saying the Cubs could not compete for the pennant, that they were a "second division team." Cavarretta promptly acquired the distinction of being the first manager ever fired during spring training. He was, of course, right about the team. The Cubs' 64–90 record—their fourth season with 90 or more losses since 1948—landed them in seventh place.

William Wrigley had died in January 1932 at his winter home in Phoenix, where, with the assistance of a Chicago architect named Frank Lloyd Wright, he had built the Biltmore Hotel. The Cubs fell into the lap of his son, Philip, who in at least one way was like his father. He was a promoter. His product was baseball.

Or maybe not. The product was actually the Wrigley Field experience. His father had loved baseball; Philip never really pretended to. When, in 1934, he became the team's president, he said, "God knows, I don't want the job." By inertia he acquired responsibility for the Cubs, and because of filial piety—he had assured his dying father he would not sell the team—he kept it until his own death, in 1977. Philip's son would sell the Cubs to the *Chicago Tri-*

1948: *Annus horribilis. Et tu,* Norman Rockwell?

bune in 1981. Carefully parse the words Philip said publicly after his father's death: "The club and the park stand as memorials to my father. I will never dispose of my holdings in the club as long as the chewing gum business remains profitable enough to retain it." He did not expect the team itself to be profitable. He seems to have expected it to be a loser financially as well as athletically.

Some people buy major league baseball teams as a ticket to celebrity. Wrigley, a painfully shy man, endured his inheritance. In 1958, Wrigley told *Sports Illustrated,* "I don't think I've ever done anything I've wanted to do or ever will." So determined was he to fade into the background of life that he tried to avoid being photographed. "My ambition," he said "is to go live in a cave somewhere with no telephone and roll a big rock over the door." He was commonly called P.K., which he detested because there was a brand of Wrigley gum called P.K. He insisted, implausibly, that it was named not for him but because a Wrigley gum slogan was "Packed tight, kept right."

Born on December 5, 1894, he was sent to a tony prep school, Andover. He was, his father hoped and assumed, destined for Yale. Instead, Philip left Andover before graduating and entered the family business, running the Wrigley chewing-gum factory in Australia. An able businessman, he had also inherited his father's faith in advertising. And he had, as many people successful in business do, inordinate faith in his expertise beyond his core business. His business was chewing gum. Baseball was a hobby. And it was not his favorite hobby, which was tinkering with motors.

Charlie Grimm, who played for the Cubs for twelve seasons and who managed them for P. K. Wrigley four times, said that concerning baseball, Wrigley was "absolutely wrong about everything." For example, Wrigley's 1938 brainstorm was to hire a University of Illinois professor to measure the reflexes and physical characteristics of the Cubs' players, who were not amused. "It was," Wrigley said, "a coincidence that he was the head of the psychology department."

Loyalty to a Chicago friend caused Wrigley to resist the

P. K. Wrigley, reluctant owner.

newfangled idea of farm teams, where talent could be cul-
tivated. Wrigley's father was among those who recruited
Judge Kenesaw Mountain Landis to be baseball commissioner, and Landis, said the younger Wrigley, was opposed
to farm systems: "Because of our high regard for the Judge,
we had no farm system."

When World War II military conscription depleted
the major league rosters, Wrigley was the prime mover behind the creation of the All-American Girls Professional

Baseball League. This venture inspired the 1992 movie *A League of Their Own*, in which Tom Hanks famously says something Cub fans dispute: "There's no crying in baseball." There is, however, apologizing. An ad Wrigley placed in Chicago newspapers in 1948 read in full:

> The Cub management wants you to know we appreciate the wonderful support you are giving the ball club. We want to have a winning team that can be up at the top—the kind you deserve. This year's rebuilding job has been a flop. But we are not content to just go along with an eye to attendance. We want a winner just as you do and will do everything in our power to get one.

Not exactly. Winning was not central to P.K.'s business plan, which he explained this way: "Our idea in advertising the game, and the fun, and the healthfulness of it, the sunshine and the relaxation, is to get the public to see ballgames, win or lose." Although in 1941 he was prepared to sacrifice some sunshine for artificial light, the attack on Pearl Harbor prompted him to donate to the war effort the steel he had purchased for Wrigley Field lights. And then after the war, he seemed to revert to his 1935 belief that night baseball was "just a passing fad."

Jim Brosnan, a pitcher who wrote two books about his major league experiences, *The Long Season* and *Pennant Race*, spent four seasons with the Cubs in the mid-1950s. He said of Wrigley, "His slogan was 'Come Out and Have a Picnic'—and the other teams usually did." But Wrigley gave his full attention to cosmetic details. He told *Sports Illustrated*, "I've always preferred CHICAGO rather than CHICAGO CUBS on the uniform. CUBS ends up on the stomach, and that emphasizes it. Just CHICAGO across the chest makes them look huskier." You can't make such stuff up. Or this: He believed "we're in show business" and thought fans were being deprived of excitement because Cubs first and third basemen did not field grounders hit in foul territory. After he complained to his manager, the first and third basemen began exerting themselves to make stops that were as strenuous as they were pointless.

Dennis Eckersley is in the Hall of Fame, and his bronze plaque depicts him wearing an Oakland A's hat. What sort of people traded him from the Cubs to Oakland in 1987? One of the members of the Cubs' senior leadership at that time was Salty Saltwell, who P. K. Wrigley, in one of his last acts as team owner, made general manager in 1976. A year earlier, Saltwell had been in charge of Wrigley Field concessions. Buying hot dogs, selling players—what's the difference?

In 1958, Wrigley explained why he was prepared to sacrifice the family name:

> The idea is to get out in the open air, have a picnic. We mention that the things people like to do, to enjoy, are all in the ballpark. We stress the green vines on the wall. We stopped calling it Wrigley Field. Instead we call it Cubs Park. You

see, people want to go to a park. We are aiming
at people not interested in baseball. These are
fans we want to get. Dyed-in-the-wool fans want
us to tell about batting averages. Why should we
tell the dyed-in-the-wool fans? They know where
everything is, what's going on.

There you have it. Much of the Cubs' history is explained by the celebration of Wrigley Field—or, if you
prefer, Cubs Park—as a haven for "people not interested
in baseball."

*A doctor can bury his mistakes, but an architect
can only advise his clients to plant vines.*
—FRANK LLOYD WRIGHT

It is not a good sign for fans when their team's venue is better known for the attractiveness of its flora than for the excellence of the athletes who have played there. Which
brings us to the subject of Wrigley Field's ivy.

Its origin story is told by Bill Veeck Jr. with characteristic verve, and perhaps equally characteristic license, in his
autobiography *Veeck as in Wreck*, one of the indispensable
books for any baseball fan's library. In 1917, when Wrigley
Field and Bill were both three years old, his father, Wil-

The ivy arrives in September 1937.

liam Veeck Sr., became president of the Chicago Cubs. He had written several articles for the *Chicago American* in a literary genre that has, by now, a long tradition—the What Is Wrong with the Cubs? school of analysis. Veeck Sr. had explained, frequently and perhaps a bit obnoxiously, what he would do were he running the franchise. The team's owner, William Wrigley, said, in effect: Well, then, smarty-pants, come aboard and do it.

Which Veeck did for sixteen years, during which, his son was to write, the Cubs won their first pennant in twenty-one years. (Bill Jr. was mistaken: The Cubs won in 1929, just eleven years after their previous pennant.) Bill Jr. also wrote that under his father the Cubs became the first major league team to draw a million fans in a season. He was wrong again. In 1927, the Cubs became the first

National League team to draw more than a million, but the Yankees had done that in 1920, with 1,289,422. The Cubs' 1927 attendance of 1,159,168 was, however, the record for a Chicago team until the Cubs drew 1,485,166 two years later. The Cubs held the Chicago record until 1960, when the White Sox drew 1,644,460 under the ownership of . . . Bill Veeck Jr.

But we are getting ahead of the story.

At age ten, Bill, who attended school with the sons of Ring Lardner, a star sportswriter for the *Chicago American*, began accompanying his father to the ballpark. By the time he was fifteen, his duties included mailing out tickets for Ladies' Day games, and P.K. hired him as an office boy, paying him eighteen dollars a week. The younger Wrigley was not a great builder of Cub teams, but as Veeck says, "He made the park itself his best promotion." In doing so, "he taught me perhaps the greatest single lesson of running a ball club." This lesson, which might be one reason why the Cubs have been so badly run, was explained by Veeck this way:

Wrigley compared the Cubs' won-and-lost records with corresponding daily-attendance charts and showed me that the two followed a practically identical pattern. His conclusion was inescapable. A team that isn't winning a pennant has to sell something in addition to its won-lost record to fill in those low points on the attendance chart. His solution was to sell "Beautiful Wrigley Field"; that is, to make the park itself so great an attraction that it would be thought of as a place to take the whole family for a delightful day.

This became the Cubs' conscious business model: If the team is bad, strive mightily to improve . . . the ballpark. In that spirit, Veeck got Wrigley's permission to install atop the flagpole on the center-field scoreboard a crossbar with a green light on one side and a red light on the other, visible to passengers heading home on the elevated trains in the late afternoon. The green light announced a victory, the red a defeat. But neither victory nor defeat mattered as much as the venue for both.

Pursuant to Wrigley's plan to have a beautiful setting for ugly baseball, Veeck suggested that they borrow an idea from Perry Stadium, in Indianapolis, where ivy adorned the outfield walls. Wrigley responded enthusiastically, "And we can put trees or something in the back." Except he did not want the trees outside the park; he wanted them in the bleachers. And although Wrigley seems to have had too much patience when trying, sort of, to grow a good team, he did not want to wait for saplings to grow big enough to shade the steps leading up to the scoreboard. So tree boxes large enough for full-grown trees were built on each step. These required concrete footings, which, in turn, required new steel supports for the bleachers, to withstand the weight. The trees were planted and, Veeck recalled, "a week after we were finished the bleachers looked like the Russian steppes during a hard, cold winter. Nothing but cement and bark." The wind off Lake Michigan had stripped the leaves from the trees. So new trees were planted. And the wind again denuded them. The forestation of the Wrigley Field bleachers was eventually abandoned. The footings for the trees had cost $200,000. That year, 1937, the Cubs' team payroll was about $250,000.

Veeck had planned to plant the ivy after the season. However, the day before the team returned from a long road trip to end the season with a short home stand, Wrigley told Veeck he had invited some friends to the next day's game to see the ivy. But Veeck had not yet bought it. A specialist at a nursery was consulted. He said ivy could not be deployed in one night. Veeck asked what could be. The specialist answered with one word: "Bittersweet." He was not a philosophic merchant commenting on the human condition; neither was he summing up the experience of being a Cub fan. Rather, he was recommending a plant with that name. So that night Veeck and Wrigley Field's groundskeeper strung light bulbs along the outfield wall to illuminate their work, and by morning the wall was entirely covered with bittersweet. In its midst they planted ivy, which eventually took over the wall.

Veeck was also involved in installing something that today is still very much what it was then: the green hand-operated scoreboard. The designer of this had a dreadful idea. Veeck wrote, "Instead of having lights switching on and off, like all other scoreboards, his model featured brightly painted eyelids which were pulled up and down magnetically." Cub fans, who have been spared so few embarrassments, were spared this one.

Veeck went on to own the St. Louis Browns, from 1951 through 1953. That team frequently played in front of such small crowds that Veeck used to joke that when a fan called to ask what time that day's game would start, he would answer, "What time can you get here?" The ivy he planted probably drew more fans to Wrigley Field than his Browns team drew to Sportsman's Park in St. Louis.

On September 17, 1937, the *Chicago Tribune* carried a story with this headline: "New Wrigley Field Blooms in Scenic Beauty—and Scoffers Rush to Apologize." One of the scoffers was the author of the story, Edward Burns, who had written a series of grumpy reports about changes under way at the field, including enlargement of the bleachers. Now, however, he was prepared to "emboss an apologetic scroll to P. K. Wrigley, owner of the most artistic ballpark in the majors." Burns estimated that the park was valued at $3 million.

Paul Dickson is the author of a 2012 biography of Veeck that contains some fascinating details about Veeck's job supervising Wrigley Field's concessions. Veeck hired vendors to sell programs, peanuts, and other ballpark staples, and one of his hires was known as a "duker," meaning a sort of hustler. This young fellow, named Jacob Leon Rubenstein, had been born in 1911 and had developed some disagreeable tricks of the vendor's trade, such as bumping into a startled fan, placing the program in his hand, and then demanding a quarter in payment. Rubenstein also hawked paper birds tied to wooden sticks. The birds chirped when the sticks were twirled, and he would foist them on children in the hope that they would pressure their parents into purchasing the birds. Veeck said the Cubs assigned someone with binoculars to monitor this vendor "to make sure they were getting their share of his nefarious sales."

This vendor did not linger in Chicago. Rubenstein went west, changing his name to Jack Ruby. In 1947, he settled in Dallas, where he opened several seedy nightclubs. On November 22, 1963, distraught about the assassination of President John Kennedy, the former vendor put his snub-nosed Colt Cobra .38-caliber revolver in his jacket pocket and headed to the Dallas police headquarters, where Oswald was being held; there, he passed himself off as a newspaper reporter to attend a press conference about the assassination. Two days later, he returned to that building and fatally shot Lee Harvey Oswald. Ruby was convicted of murder with malice and sentenced to death. His conviction was overturned, and he succumbed to lung cancer while awaiting a new trial. He died at Parkland Hospital, where Kennedy had been declared dead, and where Oswald had died from Ruby's gunshot. Ruby is buried in Westlawn Cemetery in Norridge, Illinois, nine miles from Wrigley Field.

Veeck's supervision of Wrigley Field's concessions also brought him into contact with a short, stocky go-getter salesman of paper cups and Multimixer milk-shake machines. The salesman was an ardent Cub fan. He was also a pest, constantly badgering Veeck to stock up on more cups. Born in 1902 in Oak Park, Illinois, Ray Kroc was a cheerful Willy Loman. The son of immigrants from Czechoslovakia, he was as unpretentious as a hamburger, as salty as a French fry, and as American as frozen apple pie. In 1945, after sixteen years of the Depression and war, Americans were eager to get into their cars and hit the road, which is what Kroc did to hawk his cups and machines. In 1954, when he got an astonishing order for eight milk-shake machines from a restaurant in San Bernardino, California, owned by two brothers, he went there to take a look. One look was all he needed.

The Second World War had accustomed many millions of American palates to the standardized fare of C-rations and factory canteens. Standardization was what the San Bernardino brothers offered. Kroc convinced Richard and Maurice McDonald to accept a small percentage of his gross revenues, if there were to be any, in exchange for his use of their name and business model, which involved selling only hamburgers (fifteen cents), fries (ten cents), and milk shakes (twenty cents). He opened his first restaurant in Des Plaines, a Chicago suburb fifteen miles from Wrigley Field. By the time he died, in 1984, he had satisfied his baseball yearnings by buying the San Diego Padres. As Wrigley Field turns one hundred, there are more than thirty-four thousand McDonald's restaurants worldwide.

Paul Sullivan, who has been covering baseball for the *Chicago Tribune* since 1989 and has been working for the paper since 1981, remembers that "in the early 1980s,

Veeck used to hang out at Wrigley Field." When Veeck sold the White Sox, in 1981, he thought the new owners disparaged his years on the South Side, so he returned to Wrigley Field to slake his undiminished thirst for baseball. And for beer. "He could drink like a fish," Sullivan recalls, "but never had to go to the bathroom." It was, Sullivan says, as though Veeck's wooden leg—a war wound, then thirty-six surgeries, cost him a leg—were hollow. It wasn't, but it did have a slide-out ashtray, which was cheeky for a man with cancer. But, then, insouciance was the essence of Veeck, the baseball lifer who one night in 1937 gave Wrigley Field the look that to this day defines it. Late in his life he used to sit high above the ivy he had planted, in the upper part of the center-field bleachers. These years were, Sullivan says with a tone of some regret, "the last gasp of the old Wrigley Field." He means that those were the last days before the fans, their appetite for success whetted by the 1984 season, began to become impatient for wins. Before that, says Sullivan, "The team was bad and the fans weren't that bothered by it."

Bill Veeck's winding baseball trail took him back to where he began. He died in 1986. He was cremated, and his ashes are in Oak Woods Cemetery, fifteen miles from Wrigley Field. He is spending eternity in interesting company. Also buried there, in addition to Chicago gangsters Big Jim Colosimo and Jake "Greasy Thumb" Guzik, are Jesse Owens, the hero of the 1936 Berlin Olympics, and Commissioner Kenesaw Mountain Landis.

In 1919, two years after the Russian Revolution announced the agenda of abolishing private property, William Wrigley bought a fifty-eight-thousand-acre island. Santa Catalina, the "isle with the smile," is about twenty miles off California's Orange County. The Cubs conducted spring training on the island from 1921 until shifting to Mesa, Arizona, in 1951. That, however, is not why Santa Catalina deserves an important paragraph in American history. Here is why:

Ronald Wilson Reagan of Dixon, Illinois, graduated from Eureka College in Eureka, Illinois, in 1932, the trough of the Depression. The unemployment rate was 26 percent when he hitchhiked home to Dixon, where he applied for a $12.50-a-week job managing the sporting goods section of a store Montgomery Ward was opening there. The job went to one of his high school classmates, which was a fortunate failure for Reagan, who set out in his family's car to seek employment as a radio announcer. After a brief and rocky stint with WOC in Davenport, Iowa, where he was miscast as a disc jockey, he was offered a chance to broadcast the Drake Relays, one of the nation's premier track meets, for station WHO in Des Moines. The station liked what it heard and made Reagan a sportscaster; his tasks included re-creating Cubs games as details trickled in

yours For Kentucky Winners and Kentucky Club. Dutch Reagan

Dapper Dutch: Santa Catalina Island, here I come.

over a telegraph wire. In 1937, Reagan persuaded the station to finance his drive to southern California to report about the Cubs' spring training on Santa Catalina Island. He had dinner in Los Angeles with a former WHO colleague, who put him in touch with an agent, who placed the famous call to a casting director at Warner Bros.: "I have another Robert Taylor sitting in my office."

The unimpressed director supposedly replied that God made only one Robert Taylor. Nevertheless, Reagan got his foot in Hollywood's door. When he was still twenty-eight years away from winning the presidency, he starred in the 1952 movie *The Winning Team*, playing a former Cubs pitcher with a presidential name: Grover Cleveland Alex-

A right-hander on the Wrigley Field mound.

ander, who, like Reagan, was the son of an alcoholic. Alexander suffered from alcoholism and epilepsy, a bad combination, but not bad enough to prevent him from winning 373 games—128 of them for the Cubs—and becoming, in 1938, a member of the third class elected to the Hall of Fame.

In his 1990 memoir, *An American Life*, Reagan wrote, "At twenty-two I'd achieved my dream: I was a sports announcer. If I had stopped there, I believe I would have been happy the rest of my life." His talent for happiness is apparent in the page 95 photo of him on Wrigley Field's pitcher's mound.

The Midwest has supplied the two longest-serving commissioners of baseball: the first and the ninth, Judge Kenesaw Mountain Landis and Allan H. "Bud" Selig. Between them, they governed the sport, through 2013, for forty-six years—Landis for twenty-four and Selig for twenty-two—and they did so from the Midwest.

Landis grew up in Logansport, Indiana, and earned his law degree from what is now Northwestern University Law School. When he was commissioner, the door of his Michigan Avenue office, which was about a mile south of the Wrigley Building, had a sign of majestic terseness:

"Baseball." With his chiseled features; unsmiling, mail-slot mouth; and shock of white hair, Landis looked like a pewter statue of the virtue Rectitude. The fact that he governed like Lenin—more decisively than justly—mattered less than his visage. After baseball's trauma of the 1919 Black Sox scandal, the baseball owners hired Landis to look stern, which he often did from the front row of the box seats at Wrigley Field, not far from where Al Capone occasionally sat.

Selig, a native of Milwaukee, has been the un-Landis. He is never autocratic, and he has a genius for the politics of a small group—the thirty owners. No one really knows how Selig has made many of his decisions or how he has produced support for them among those thirty fractious constituents. Like Dwight Eisenhower, Selig practices hidden-hand leadership. What is not hidden is its effectiveness. It has transformed Major League Baseball from a $1.2 billion business in 1992, when he became acting commissioner, to what probably will be a $8 billion business in Wrigley Field's one hundredth year. Selig has a posh corner office in Major League Baseball's headquarters on Park Avenue in Manhattan, but he rarely uses it. He prefers his office on the thirtieth floor of a Milwaukee bank building overlooking Lake Michigan, less than ninety miles from Wrigley Field, where in 1944 he saw his first major league game. He was a Cub fan until the Braves arrived in Milwaukee from Boston in 1953, when he began rooting for the home team. A good choice, that. The Braves won the World Series in 1957. Cub fans are still waiting.

Scott Joplin, an African American, was born soon after the end of the Civil War, in Texarkana, Arkansas, on the border with Texas. He became a traveling musician proficient in the rising style called ragtime and played with a band at the Chicago World's Fair in 1893. In 1907, when the Cubs ruled the roost in baseball, Scott Joplin lived in Chicago, where piano players in bars and bordellos probably played his 1899 composition "The Ragtime Dance":

> I attended a ball last Thursday night,
> Given by the dark town swells.
> Every coon came out in full dress alright,
> And the girls were society belles.
> The hall was illuminated by electric lights,
> It certainly was a sight to see;
> So many colored folks there without a razor
>   fight.
> 'Twas a great surprise to me.

It is stunning to become acquainted, more than a century later, with such evidence of how thoroughly American culture was permeated with an unself-conscious crudeness about race, on both sides of the racial divide. Of all the serrated edges Chicago had at the turn of the last century, none was more jagged than relations between blacks and whites.

Chicago's first resident was probably Jean Baptiste Point du Sable, who in 1779 built a trading post at the mouth of what is now known as the Chicago River. *Du Sable* means "black," and the trader was black. But 140 years later, the ugliest episode in Chicago's history occurred when a black teenager crossed a line that was difficult to see because it was drawn on water.

On July 27, 1919, Eugene Williams was swimming in Lake Michigan off the 25th Street beach, which was north of the 29th Street beach. By an unwritten social consensus, the former was for African Americans, the latter for whites. When Williams swam, probably inadvertently, south of the understood line, some whites began throwing rocks at him. It is unknown whether he drowned because a rock knocked him unconscious or because he was afraid to come ashore in white territory and was too tired to swim back to black territory.

Chicago was dry tinder that summer. Since July 1917, at least twenty-six black homes in previously all-white neighborhoods had been bombed. In the summer of 1919, a new African American newspaper, the *Whip*, had just been born, proclaiming this message:

> *The Whip* informs you, the whites, that the com-
> promising, peace-at-any-price Negro is rapidly
> passing into the scrap heap of yesterday and
> being replaced by a fearless, intelligent Negro

who recognizes no compromise but who demands absolute justice and fair play. . . . WE ARE NOT PACIFISTS, THEREFORE WE BELIEVE IN WAR, BUT ONLY WHEN ALL ORDERLY CIVIL PROCEDURE HAS BEEN EXHAUSTED AND THE POINTS IN QUESTION ARE JUSTIFIABLE. . . . THE BOMBERS WILL BE BOMBED.

The rioting that ensued after Eugene Williams drowned lasted for seven days and required the intervention of the state militia—because the city police force was too weak and too sympathetic to the rioting whites. By the end of the violence, arson, shootings, and beatings, almost all on the South Side, had resulted in 38 dead (15 whites and 23 blacks) and 537 injured (195 whites, 342 blacks).

A long fuse had burned before this explosion. For hundreds of thousands of rural blacks in the South, the Illinois Central had been the steel highway to the promised land, a.k.a. Chicago. They boarded trains at small depots in Mississippi and elsewhere and stepped off in the city's cavernous Twelfth Street station. Then they turned south, where trouble awaited them.

The First World War had accelerated the Great Migration of people escaping from American apartheid and reaching for employment in northern industries. The war. had also virtually halted housing construction. And neighborhoods of unmeltable ethnics were not welcoming. The seventeen-year-old Richard J. Daley, who would grow up to be mayor of Chicago for twenty-one years (1955–1976), lived in the South Side neighborhood of Bridgeport. There he belonged to a neighborhood club called the Hamburgs, many of whose members participated in the rioting. Did Daley join in? He was frequently asked this question but never answered it.

When Chicago was incorporated, under Illinois law, in 1837, it had approximately 3,000 residents. Thirty-four years later, at the time of the great fire of 1871, the city's population had burgeoned to 300,000 and the place was combustible in several senses. Its buildings were made of wood cut from timber harvested from the forests of Minnesota, Wisconsin, and Michigan and floated to Chicago. It was also a simmering stew of mutually suspicious ethnic communities. If the city was to become a true community, it needed some shared allegiances that would transcend ethnicity and, especially, race. Baseball could help. It finally did, but not until twenty-eight years after Eugene Williams drowned.

On Monday, May 19, 1947, the eight-column headline across the front page of the *Chicago Tribune's* sports section proclaimed:

RECORD 46,572
SEE DODGERS BEAT CUBS, 4–2

Why had so many people flocked to Wrigley Field to see the Cubs lose their fifth in a row? The story's first two paragraphs explained this in a notably understated way:

The largest National League crowd that ever paid to see a game in Wrigley Field—46,572 cash guests—yesterday jammed all available spaces to see Jackie Robinson, his fellow Dodgers and the Cubs. Those who were rooting to the Dodgers as a team got the greatest satisfaction for the Dodgers won, 4–2, with little help from Robinson and much help from the Cubs.

The crowd, by the way, was the second-largest in the history of Wrigley Field for a league game, being topped only by the gathering of 51,556 in 1930, under the old bleacher setup, when overflow field crowds were tolerated. That crowd, however, included 30,476 ladies day crasherettes.

It is difficult to decipher what the writer might have had in mind with that last word, but the 46,572 paying customers on May 18, 1947, were luckier than the 20,000 or so fans who milled around outside Wrigley Field, unable to get in. Estimates at the time were that about half of those who were drawn to Wrigley Field by Robinson's magnetism were African Americans. If so, it was probably the largest concentration of African Americans in the history of the North Side up to that point. No unpleasant incidents were reported.

The headline in the *Chicago Defender*, the paper published by and for African Americans, was:

The unruly.

ROBINSON MAKES CHICAGO DEBUT; FANS ARE ORDERLY.

A Cub official told the paper that this was "the most orderly large crowd in the history of Wrigley Field. We . . . were pleased to note that the Negro fans behaved better than our average Sunday fans, for which we thank the *Defender* for its part in this." As happened in all the cities the Dodgers visited in 1947, Chicago's African American leaders urged members of their community to dress and behave impeccably when going out with the crowd to see Robinson.

On October 24, 1972, twenty-five years after his major league debut, Jackie Robinson died. That day, Mike

Royko, the Pulitzer Prize–winning Chicago columnist, wrote about Robinson's first game at Wrigley Field. Royko said he was there, and he recalled that in 1947 "few blacks were seen in the Loop, much less up on the white North Side at a Cub game." On the day of Robinson's first visit to Wrigley Field, Royko remembered seeing something that was, indeed, common when the Dodgers visited a city that year: African American fans came to the game dressed as though for church: "white shirts, ties, gleaming shoes, and straw hats." Royko, who was then fourteen, could not get a seat but found a place to stand behind the last row of grandstand seats. He remembered that when Robinson, who was batting second, approached the plate in the first inning, there was "long, rolling applause" but that when he stepped into the batter's box, "it was as if someone had flicked a switch. The place went silent."

Late in the game, Royko said, something miraculous happened. Robinson hit a foul ball that "came into the stands low and fast, in our direction. Somebody in the seats grabbed for it, but it caromed off his hands and kept coming." Through the forest of fans' hands "the ball kept bouncing" and—you guessed it—came to rest in Royko's little hands. Royko said he sold it for ten dollars to an African American man standing next to him.

Well. Stand in Wrigley Field anywhere "behind the last row of grandstand seats" and estimate how likely it was that a foul ball got there, bouncing through the hands of some of the 46,572 other spectators there that day and finally coming into the possession, briefly and conveniently, of a future columnist. For Robinson's foul ball to have had that trajectory, the laws of physics would have to have been suspended.

Baseball is as encrusted with clichés as old ships are with barnacles. One cliché is that baseball is a game of failure. You know: In any given year, the best team will walk off the field beaten about sixty times. Ty Cobb, who had the highest career batting average (.367) in the game's history, still failed 63 percent of the time. And so on. Wrigley Field has been the scene of some notably peculiar responses to failure. When a team lacks power hitters and timely hitting, when the pitching is spotty and the defense is leaky, what do you do? You do what can be done quickly: You fire the manager. This usually fixes nothing, but it gives the illusion of purposefulness and forward motion.

In 1960, the Cubs won 60 games and lost 94; this was the seventh time in thirteen seasons they had lost at least 90 games. They finished seventh, ahead of only the 59-and-95 Phillies. Seventeen games into the 1960 season, the Cubs had fired manager Charlie Grimm and replaced him with Lou Boudreau. Although at the time Boudreau was hired he was broadcasting the Cubs' games over WGN, he had been the shortstop and player-manager of the 1948 Cleveland Indians, who won the World Series. Grimm was sent to the broadcasting booth, where he was dreadful. After the season, P. K. Wrigley, undeterred by the fact that the Cubs had tried six managers in ten seasons, decided to really, seriously change managers. Boudreau went back to broadcasting, and in came the "College of Coaches."

Has there ever in the rich history of Major League Baseball been a sillier idea than the one the Cubs adopted in 1961? That season was one of the most luminous in baseball history because of the riveting competition between two Yankees teammates, Mickey Mantle and Roger Maris, in pursuit of the record Babe Ruth had set thirty-four years earlier, when he hit sixty home runs in a season. It is fortunate for the Cubs that Mantle and Maris distracted attention from Wrigley Field, where the Cubs had implemented Wrigley's harebrained experiment known as the College of Coaches.

"Managers," Wrigley said, "are expendable. I believe there should be relief managers just like relief pitchers." So, in 1961, the Cubs would not have a manager. Instead, they would have four head coaches, who would rotate through the season. They were Harry Craft, Vedie Himsl, El Tappe, and Lou Klein. Wrigley's rationale was: "The dictionary tells you a manager is the one who bosses and a coach is the one who works. We want workers." Of course, no dictionary says any such thing. Inevitably, a joke arose: The Cubs have been playing without players, so now they will try playing without a manager. The nine coaching changes during the season caused so much confusion and uncertainty that Tappe wound up in charge of 96 games, with a 42–54 record. The other three also had losing records. It follows—arithmetic is funny this way—that the Cubs had a losing record: 64–90. They finished seventh.

So, in 1962 . . . they did it again. Craft, no fool he, decamped to Houston to manage the Houston Colt .45s, an expansion team that, notwithstanding the fact that it was assembled from scraps discarded by other teams, finished six games ahead of the Cubs, who finished ninth—the first year that was possible—and lost 103 games. They were spared the ignominy of being the first National League team to finish tenth because the historically awful New York Mets, another freshly minted expansion team, lost 120 games. Seven years later, however, the Mets would have the consolation of winning the World Series.

It is altogether fitting that on July 20 in 1962, the final year of this nadir of baseball foolishness, the Cubs passed a dismal milestone. Playing the Dodgers in Wrigley Field, they lost 8–2. With that loss, the Cubs' record since taking up residence in Wrigley Field in 1916—they had defeated the Reds 7–6 in the first game there—fell below .500. It has been there ever since.

In 1963, the Cubs gave up on Wrigley's experiment but tried to save face by continuing to call the actual manager, Bob Kennedy, "head coach." He served two years, then was replaced by head coach Lou Klein.

The College of Coaches may deserve a portion of the blame for the worst trade in Cubs history. Lou Brock was a struggling twenty-five-year-old outfielder for the Cubs when, on June 15, 1964, they lost patience and sent him to the Cardinals in exchange for a pitcher, twenty-eight-year-old Ernie Broglio. Broglio, whose career would end with the Cubs after the 1966 season, had a 7–19 record with them. The Cardinals won the 1964 World Series with Brock batting .348 in a Cardinal uniform, and they won another with him in 1967. He finished with 3,023 hits and 938 stolen bases (at the time, a major league record). These numbers are on his plaque in Cooperstown. He says he might have found his talent in Wrigley Field if he had received steady attention from coaches who were not distracted by episodic managerial duties.

One—*the* one—good result of the College of Coaches is that the Cubs became the first team to have an African American coach. Buck O'Neil of the Kansas City Monarchs was thirty-seven when Jackie Robinson broke the color line, in 1947. He was too old to play in the major leagues, but he scouted for the Cubs, who made him a coach during the college era.

After the collapse of the College of Coaches, P. K. Wrigley said, in effect: No more Mr. Nice Guy. For the 1966 season, he hired Leo Durocher, who when introduced to the Chicago media said, "If no announcement has been made about what my title is, I'm making it here and now. I'm the manager. I'm not a head coach. I'm the manager." And he was a prophet, of sorts. He promptly proclaimed that the Cubs, who had finished eighth in 1965—25 games behind, with a 72–90 record—were "not an eighth-place ball club." He was right. In 1966, they finished tenth, 36 games out of first place, with a 59–103 record.

With the hiring of Durocher, climate change came to Wrigley Field. His salty memoir, published in 1975, when he was sixty-nine, is titled *Nice Guys Finish Last*. No one was more temperamentally opposed to Wrigley Field's golly-the-ivy-is-so-green-and-the-sun-is-so-warm-and-the-beer-is-so-cold-and-the-ambience-is-so-gosh-darned-*friendly*-who-cares-what-the-score-is ethos.

"Nice guys finish last" is one of the most famous statements in baseball history. But Durocher did not say quite that. One day in the 1940s, when he was managing the Dodgers, his team was taking batting practice before a game with the Giants at their Polo Grounds. There he said of the Giants, "All nice guys. They'll finish last. Nice guys. Finish last." Journalists "improved" what he'd said. *The Oxford Dictionary of Quotations* has the correct version.

"Give me," Durocher liked to say, "some scratching, diving, hungry ballplayers who come to kill you." And: "If I were playing third base and my mother were rounding third with the run that was going to beat us, I'd trip her." He said he believed in rules, because "if there weren't any rules, how could you break them?" He illustrated that philosophy by telling how in the 1930s, when he was a shortstop with the St. Louis Cardinal Gas House Gang team, he would "file his belt buckle to a sharp edge," and when a Cardinal pitcher was in a jam, he would visit the mound and scuff the ball.

Durocher, the distilled essence of everything the Wrigley Field ethos is not, disliked the man who embodied this ethos. In fact, Durocher detested Ernie Banks, one of the best players ever to wear a Cubs uniform, and unquestionably the most beloved player in the team's history. Banks liked to be loved. Durocher reveled in his role as a human cactus, which may have been the main reason P. K. Wrigley hired him.

Another reason was that the turnstiles at Wrigley Field were turning more and more slowly. In 1965, attendance had sunk to 641,361, an average of 7,727 per game, and the club had lost $1.3 million, which was real money in a year when the average player salary was $14,341 and the average team payroll was $573,640. Wrigley's business model—serve cold beer in a pretty place and the score will not matter—was not working. And it was becoming expensive.

Durocher adored P. K. Wrigley: "Simply the finest man to work for in the world. The most decent man, probably, I have ever met." Wrigley probably reciprocated Durocher's affection because in Durocher's second year, 1967, the Cubs were making money and finished third with a winning record (87–74), the first time they had finished in what was then called "the first division"—the top half of a league—since 1946. In 1968, the Cubs again finished third (84–78) but drew more than a million customers (1,043,409) for the first time since 1952. In 1969, they drew 1,674,993, breaking a franchise record that had existed since 1929. They also set a Chicago record, topping the one set by Bill Veeck's White Sox of 1960. This at a time when Wrigley Field's capacity was just 36,667 and all games were played in the afternoon; lights were still nineteen years away. The 1969 attendance record would survive until 1984, when the Cubs played in their first postseason since 1945. Yet 1969, like 1984, would not end happily.

The Cubs started the season by winning eleven of their first twelve games and on August 7 were in first place, with a nine-game lead. But August is when the first four months of the season have taken their toll in injuries and drained energy, and before the challenge of September can revive the adrenaline of a pennant contender. Durocher, then sixty-four, was more impatient than ever to win, and he would not rest his key players, who wore down just at the moment when the "Miracle Mets"—a franchise just seven seasons old—were becoming white hot.

By September 8, the Cubs' lead was down to two and a half games as they entered Shea Stadium for their final two away games against the Mets. They lost both, their slide accelerated, and they finished the season in second place, eight games behind the Mets, who went on to defeat Baltimore's heavily favored Orioles 4–1 in the World Series.

The remainder of Durocher's stay in Chicago was an exercise in disappointment, a fact that he blamed on Banks and perhaps the second-most-popular Cub of all time, third baseman Ron Santo. "Right in the middle of the lineup," Durocher complained, "I had two men who couldn't run." Durocher says he tried to trade Santo but could get no takers. What he says about Banks is scalding. He concedes that Banks was a great player in his time but adds, "Unfortunately, his time wasn't my time." Durocher knew how to nurse a grudge, and when he published his memoir, just three years after leaving the Friendly Confines, he offered an unfriendly assessment of Banks:

> He couldn't run, he couldn't field; toward the end, he couldn't even hit. There are some players who instinctively do the right thing on the base paths. Ernie had an unfailing instinct for doing the wrong thing. But I had to play him. Had to play the man or there would have been a revolution in the street. . . . Ernie Banks owns Chicago. . . . How does he do it? You could say about Ernie that he never remembered a sign or forgot a newspaperman's name.

Durocher was just warming to his theme:

> With every other player, we had the usual signs, an indicator followed by a combination. With Ernie we had to have flash signs. One sign. Like the Little League. Ernie, you're always hitting unless we flash something at you. If I tip my hat, now you're taking. Pull up my belt, it's a hit-and-run. In my first year, when he could still run a little, I'd sometimes want him moving on a 3–1 count [when he was the runner on first] with Santo at

bat to break up the possible double play. From
the bench, you could see his whole body just rear
back and he'd look at the coach as if he were saying, "You got to be kidding." Your little boy knows
that it's percentage baseball to get a runner moving on a 3–1 count under those conditions. But
not Mister Cub.

Both of Banks's knees were shot by the end of his career,
which came after the 1971 season. Durocher says, "He'd
come up with men on the bases and if he hit a ground ball
they could walk through the double play." In the field, "if
the ball wasn't hit right at him, forget it. He'd wave at it.
Two feet away from him—whoops—right under his glove."

That is the brief for the prosecution. Now for the defense.

Not that Ernie Banks needs any defense in the environs of
Wrigley Field, where a statue of him stands on Clark Street,
near the home plate entrance. He is the face of the Cubs
franchise, as much as Stan Musial, Bob Feller, Ted Williams, Robin Yount, Tony Gwynn, and Cal Ripken are the
iconic players of the Cardinals, Indians, Red Sox, Brewers,
Padres, and Orioles, respectively. Just as Wrigley Field is,
for better or worse, a summation of the Cubs' experience,

Banks embodies the post-1945 franchise, for two reasons. First, his disposition, win or lose—and it was mostly lose—was as sunny as the ballpark in which he never performed at night. Second, his play demonstrated that even in a team game, a player can achieve greatness with precious little support from his teammates.

It is odd that in the 1950s, a decade in which the Cubs' record was 672 wins and 866 losses (.437), two Cubs players won a total of three National League Most Valuable Player awards. In 1952, left fielder Hank Sauer led the league with 37 home runs and 121 runs batted in. This was four years before the Cy Young Award was created for pitchers, so pitchers were as eligible as position players to be named MVPs. Indeed, Bobby Shantz of the Philadelphia Athletics was the 1952 American League MVP, with a record of 24–7 and a 2.48 ERA. The 1952 National League award should have gone to another pitcher from that city, Robin Roberts, who had a phenomenal 28–7 record and a 2.59 ERA for a mediocre fourth-place team with a 87–67 record. Sauer won the award even though Roberts was responsible for 32 percent of his team's wins.

In 1958 and 1959, Ernie Banks won the MVP award even though in those two seasons the Cubs had a cumulative record sixteen games under .500 (72–82 and 74–80). The next player—and, as of this writing, the last NL player—to win the MVP award while playing on a team with a losing record was another Cub, right fielder Andre Dawson, who had 49 home runs and 137 RBIs with the

1987 Cubs, who finished sixth, which was last place in what was then the National League's East Division.

Banks could have been a Cardinal. In the spring of 1953, one of that team's scouts saw him playing shortstop for the Kansas City Monarchs of the Negro League and sent a favorable report to St. Louis. The Cardinals sent out another scout for a second opinion, which was: "I don't think he is a major league prospect. He can't hit, he can't run, he has a pretty good arm but it's a scatter arm. I don't like him." In the annals of misjudgments, that ranks with the report on the screen test of a young Fred Astaire: "Can't act. Slightly bald. Can dance a little."

On July 28, 1953, Hugh Wise, a scout for the Cubs, submitted the report reproduced here on page 35. On the nineteenth line down, on the right, the question is how many years it will be before Banks can play in the major leagues. Wise said: "Can play now." Forty-two days later, Banks came to the Cubs. Golenbock says that when Banks got to Wrigley Field he did not own a glove, so teammate Eddie Miksis lent him one.

The rise of the White Sox to temporary baseball supremacy in Chicago in the 1950s began in 1951, with the arrival on the South Side of Saturnino Orestes Armas Arrieta Minoso. Minnie Minoso, as he was known, was a Cuban who integrated Chicago baseball two years before Banks got to Wrigley Field. Banks came from the Monarchs in September 1953. Second baseman Gene Baker, also an African American, came to the Cubs three days later. They signed Baker partly because he was a gifted player, but also because in those days players slept two to a room on the road and it was assumed that a black player had to have a black roommate.

At that time there was, it is important to remember, uneasiness all around. When Banks had left the army, Abe Saperstein, the owner of the Harlem Globetrotters, had asked him to play with the team in a game. Banks said that when Saperstein invited him to sit down and talk about the opportunity, "I'd never sat down next to a white man, and I wasn't sure what to do." Different African Americans had different coping strategies for navigating the changing social terrain. Frank Robinson, arriving in the big leagues with the Cincinnati Reds shortly after Banks came to the Cubs, brought a prickly ferocity that served him well. Banks's unshakable, even preternatural, amiability served him even better.

Banks's signature words as a professional athlete were: "It's a beautiful day, let's play two!" But when he was a child in Dallas, his father had to bribe him with pocket change to get him to play catch. At Booker T. Washington High School in that city's segregated school system, Banks was a football, basketball, soccer, and track star. In that time and place, however, athletic proficiency was not, for an African American, a reliable ticket to a professional career. So at age seventeen, Banks began playing baseball with an African American barnstorming team that paid him fifteen dollars a game. One of the greatest black players, Cool Papa Bell, spotted Banks and signed him for the

Monarchs. Banks returned to them after being drafted into two years of service in the army, and in the summer of 1953, when Banks was twenty-two, the Cubs signed him and soon brought him to the North Side.

He had 35 at bats in 10 games, with 11 hits, 2 of them home runs. In 1954, he played in all 154 games and hit 19 home runs. Then came one of the most remarkable six years of slugging in major league history. His home run totals were:

1955	44
1956	28
1957	43
1958	47
1959	45
1960	41

His major league contemporaries in the second half of the 1950s included future Hall of Famers Mickey Mantle, Yogi Berra, Ted Williams, Willie Mays, Henry Aaron, Frank Robinson, and Duke Snider. Snider hit more home runs in the 1950s than anyone else in either league. In the second half of the decade, however, Banks hit more home runs than any of them. In 1955, the year he hit a record five grand slams, he switched to a lighter, thin-handled bat and changed the idea of what a shortstop could do at the plate.

Since the 1917 retirement of the Pirates' Honus Wagner, the greatest shortstop in baseball history, potent hitters had rarely played that position. Before Banks, no National

League shortstop had hit even 25 home runs in a season. The NL shortstop home run record was 23, by the Giants' Alvin Dark in 1953. Only one American League shortstop, Vern Stephens of the Red Sox, a right-handed hitter taking aim at Fenway Park's Green Monster wall down the short (310 feet) left-field foul line, had hit more: 29 in 1948, 39 in 1949, and 30 in 1950.

Then along came Banks, who, like Henry Aaron ninety miles north, used extraordinarily strong wrists to whip a light, thin-handled bat through the strike zone. "His wrists," said a teammate, "go right up to his armpits." Although in 1961 Banks would be moved to first base and would play more games at that position than at shortstop, he blazed the path for slugging shortstops like Cal Ripken and Alex Rodriguez. What is especially remarkable is that Banks did this when it did not make much sense for pitchers to throw him strikes.

In 1955, the most common Yankees lineup had Yogi Berra, a hard-hitting catcher, batting behind Mantle. The most common Braves lineup had future Hall of Famer Eddie Mathews (512 career home runs) batting in front of Aaron. The most common Dodgers batting order had Duke Snider batting in front of future Hall of Famer Roy Campanella, who in 1955 hit 32 of his 242 career home runs and won his third Most Valuable Player award. Who was behind Banks in the most common 1955 Cubs batting order? Ransom Jackson, a.k.a. Handsome Ransom. He hit 103 home runs in a ten-year career. Banks has been faulted for not "working the count" to get a lot of walks. But what would have been the point—to hope Jackson would drive him in? In 1959, Banks became the first National League player to win a second consecutive MVP award. In the most frequent Cubs batting order that season, he batted in front of Walt Moryn (101 home runs in eight seasons).

Bill James, in the first version of his *Historical Baseball Abstract*, published in 1985, ranked Banks the fortieth best player of all time. By the time James's 2001 version appeared, he ranked Banks seventy-seventh. James cited the fact that over his career Banks hit sixty-eight more home runs at Wrigley Field than on the road. This, James says, "makes him among the most fortunate home run hitters in history." James presumably means that Wrigley is a hitter-friendly ballpark. It certainly is when the wind is blowing out, which many people assume is the norm in the Windy City. But during the five seasons from 2008 through 2012, the wind blew in 57.4 percent of the time, it blew out 24 percent, and there were either crosswinds or no wind the rest of the time.

Were this myth a fact, it is unlikely that in 1999 the *Sporting News* would have ranked Banks thirty-eighth on its "Baseball's Greatest Players" list or that he would have been elected to the thirty-member "Major League Baseball All-Century Team."

After the Braves' third baseman Eddie Mathews, Banks was the second infielder, other than first basemen, to hit more than five hundred home runs. It is rare in baseball history that one player has been, as Banks was for a decade, the only reason—the only baseball reason—for fans to go out to see the home team. And through it all, Banks was unfailingly cheerful. (To someone with Durocher's sensibilities, Banks was maddeningly cheerful.)

Banks's record of five grand slam home runs in a season was broken when the Yankees' Don Mattingly hit six in 1987. So the only major league record Banks still holds is 2,528 games played without ever appearing in postseason competition. But through it all he played hard. Look again at the 1953 scouting report on Banks. Note the right side of the ninth line down, the space for assessing "attitude." Scout Hugh Wise said: "Very good." Quite right. In 1958, an opposing manager, Jimmy Dykes, noted, "Without Ernie Banks, the Cubs would finish in Albuquerque." True enough.

On March 31, 2008, the statue of Banks in his upright stance, his bat almost perfectly perpendicular to the ground, was unveiled at Wrigley Field. The inscription on the base read, "Lets play two." Two days later, the sculptor came to Wrigley early in the morning and added an apostrophe.

Getting things not quite right is something of a tradition around Wrigley Field. Another statue outside the ballpark is of broadcaster Harry Caray, who sang "Take Me Out to the Ball Game" during thousands of Wrigley Field seventh-inning stretches and almost always sang it wrong.

He sang "take me out to the crowd" rather than "with the crowd" and "I don't care if I ever get back" rather than "if I never get back." It was almost as though even off-the-field errors somehow authenticated the Wrigley Field experience. Caray was one of three famous baseball people to come from the Italian section of St. Louis. The other two were catchers: Joe Garagiola, who had a better career in broadcasting than as a player, and Yogi Berra. In 1945, Caray became the radio play-by-play broadcaster for the Cardinals and, briefly, for the St. Louis Browns, too. In 1953, the Cardinals were bought by August Busch II of the Budweiser brewery dynasty. According to Golenbock, Caray was fired by the Cardinals in 1969 for a reason that never became public knowledge:

> Detectives hired by the Busch family discovered a string of telephone calls from Harry to the wife of August Busch III, Gussie's son. They intuited that Harry, whose reputation for drinking and partying was legendary, was having an affair with this woman. Harry never denied it. All he said was, "I never raped anyone in my life."

Having broadcast Cardinals games for twenty-five years, Caray did Oakland A's games for the 1970 season, then moved to the Chicago White Sox for eleven seasons. He moved to the North Side for the 1982 season, and the WGN superstation made him a national celebrity, perhaps second only to Ernie Banks as emblematic of Wrigley Field.

Nearly forty years after he first experienced it, Mike Krukow, now in his third decade of broadcasting San Francisco Giants games, still fondly recalls the unique pleasure of playing at Wrigley Field. In a successful fourteen-year pitching career (124 wins, 117 losses), he spent his first five full seasons with the Cubs. The night before his first day as a big leaguer—September 6, 1976—he slept fitfully. In the morning, he rose early, grabbed his equipment bag bearing the logo of his last minor league team, the Wichita Aeros, and stepped out of his hotel and into a cab. "I said to the driver the two words I had been waiting all my life to say: 'Wrigley Field.' She said: 'How do I get there?'"

He got there, was given a uniform with the number 40, and stepped out into the Friendly Confines to stretch and run sprints. While he was jogging with a Cub veteran, a fan in the bleachers began shouting, "Hey, Forty, what's your name, man?" After a few such shouts, the Cub veteran told Krukow, "Just tell him to buy a program." So the next time Krukow ran past the fan and the fan repeated his shout, Krukow yelled back, "Go buy a program, meat." To which the fan replied, "I did—and you ain't in it." After that, Krukow told the Cubs' clubhouse man, "Give me any number but fucking 40." He became number 39.

That first day at Wrigley Field, Krukow was told there

was already a president of the Krukow Fan Club. He recalls that every Cub, no matter how new or obscure, had a fan club—the membership of which consisted, he says, of all the presidents of the other players' fan clubs. He'd been paid $1,050 a month in Wichita, and in Chicago the next year he made the major league minimum—about $22,500, as he recalls it. He could not afford to live in the city, so he had to commute from the suburbs. Since all the games took place during the day, he was in rush hour both ways. Today he says, with mock indignation, "It was like you had a *job*." But because Cub players were so special in the city, he earned $500 for each of three personal appearances, which was serious money in those days before baseball became rich.

In 1981, his last season with the Cubs, they were so dreadful (38–65), he believes that if a players' strike had not shortened the season, the Cubs might have broken the 1962 New York Mets' record of 120 losses. More than three decades later, he seems almost wistful about the missed opportunity.

Because Krukow pitched on May 13, 1979, he missed a chance to play in one of the most memorable games in Wrigley Field's history. On May 17, the ballpark lived up to—or perhaps down to—its reputation as a purgatory for pitchers. The major league record for runs scored in a game had been set there fifty-seven years earlier, on August 25, 1922, when the Cubs defeated the Phillies 26–23. That record still stands, but the Cubs and the Phillies made a valiant effort at topping it on May 17, 1979.

The game began with Dennis Lamp on the mound—
briefly—for the home team. He lasted a third of an inning.
Before he could get the second out of the first inning, he
surrendered two home runs. Two three-run home runs. As
his wife settled into her seat in the top of the first, she said,
"Where is he?" He was already licking his wounds in the
clubhouse, where he would soon be joined by a succession
of shell-shocked pitchers as the farce unfolded over four
hours and three minutes. The Cubs came to bat in the bottom of the first trailing 7–0. They finished the first inning
trailing 7–6.

A Phillies broadcaster that day, and for several decades
more, was Richie Ashburn. He had a Hall of Fame career
as the Phillies' center fielder for twelve seasons, and toward
the end of his fifteen-year career he played two seasons
with the Cubs, who had a tradition of acquiring future
Hall of Fame players after they had expended most of their
greatness elsewhere (see, for example, Dizzy Dean, Ralph
Kiner, Robin Roberts). In Ashburn's final big league season, when he was voted the most valuable player on the
1962 Mets, an expansion team that lost 120 games, he said,
"MVP on the worst team ever? I wonder what exactly they
meant by that?" So Ashburn was familiar with bizarre
baseball, and with Wrigley Field when the wind was gust-
ing out. It was doing so at eighteen miles per hour on May
17, 1979. During the first inning Ashburn said, "I have a
feeling this might wind up about 19–12." He was off by
fourteen runs.

By the time the Phillies finished circling the bases in

the fifth inning, they led 21–9, and Ashburn's scorecard was, he said, "uncipherable." It was a day that demanded such a neologism. The Cubs scored seven in the bottom half of the fifth inning, turning the game into a 21–16 squeaker. By the end of nine, the score was 22–22. The Phillies drove in their twenty-third and winning run in the top of the tenth. The losing pitcher, the Cubs' sixth pitcher of the game, was a future Hall of Famer, Bruce Sutter, who would win the Cy Young Award that year and who, true to another Cub tradition, had begun his career with the Cubs but entered the Hall of Fame wearing another team's cap (see Lou Brock of the Cardinals and Greg Maddux of the Braves). The last out of the game was made when future Hall of Famer Mike Schmidt, who hit two home runs that day, fielded a grounder and threw to the first baseman, Pete Rose, who, were it not for his unfortunate habit of betting on baseball, would be in the Hall of Fame. It is somehow fitting that the Phillies' manager in 1979 was Danny Ozark, who was given to mind-bending thoughts such as, "Even Napoleon had his Watergate" and "Contrary to popular belief, I have always had a wonderful repertoire with my players." He was not talking about the 23–22 game, but he could have been when he said, "It is beyond my apprehension." He once remarked of baseball, "Half this game is 90 percent mental." Less than half on May 17, 1979.

On that day, Krukow remembers, "I was charting." As was standard practice, the previous day's pitcher charted both teams' pitches, of which there were about five hundred as the two teams piled up fifty hits (Phillies 24, Cubs 26),

the fourth most in baseball since 1900. Exaggerating somewhat, Krukow now says, "I wore out three pens and had to
go on the DL with a broken wrist." As was something of a
Wrigley Field tradition, the baseball that day made up in
entertainment value what it lacked in artistry.

April is—a poet born and raised in the Midwest said so—
the cruelest month. In 1983, it was especially not nice on
the North Side. The Cubs staggered out of the starting
gate, and there was noisy disapproval from the few fans
who were drawn to the Friendly Confines in the often unfriendly weather of a Chicago spring. On April 29, 9,391
fans filed out of Wrigley Field after the Cubs lost to the Los
Angeles Dodgers, 4–3. Cub manager Lee Elia was in his
office after the game, with the media present, their pens
and voice recorders in hand. They would not be disap-
pointed by his colorful meditation on Cub fans.

Then forty-five, Elia was a baseball journeyman whose
most memorable contribution to the game's lore was about
to occur. It became an instant classic of a particular genre
of expression, the Postgame Rant. It is available, and probably will be through eternity, in the digital ether. Because
it is the most famous rhetorical moment in Wrigley Field
history, it is here reprinted, with excisions made to protect
the delicate sensibilities of readers:

"I'll tell you one f**kin' thing, I hope we get f**kin' hotter than s**t, just to stuff it up them three thousand f**kin' people that show up every f**kin' day because if they're the real Chicago f**kin' fans, they can kiss my f**kin' ass right downtown—and print it! They're really, really behind you around here—my f**kin' ass. What the f**k am I supposed to do, go out there and let my f**kin' players get destroyed every day and be quiet about it? For the f**kin' nickel-dime people that show up? The motherf**kers don't even work. That's why they're out at the f**kin' game. They ought to go out and get a f**kin' job and find out what it's like to go out and earn a f**kin' living. Eighty-five percent of the f**kin' world is working. The other fifteen come out here. A f**kin' playground for the c*********s. Rip them motherf**kers. Rip them f**kin' c******kers like the f**kin' players. We got guys bustin' their f**kin' ass, and them f**kin' people boo. And that's the Cubs? My f**kin' ass. They talk about the great f**kin' support that the players get around here. I haven't seen it this f**kin' year. . . . The name of the game is hit the ball, catch the ball and get the f**kin' job done. Right now we have more losses than we have wins. So f**kin' changes that have happened in the Cubs organization are multifold.

All right, they don't show because we're five and fourteen—and unfortunately that's the criteria of them dumb fifteen motherf**kin' percent that come out to day baseball. The other eighty-five percent are earning a living. It'll take more than a five-and-thirteener, five and fourteen to destroy the makeup of this club. I guarantee you that. There's some f**kin' pros out there that wanna f**kin' play this game. But you're stuck in a f**kin' stigma of the f**kin' Dodgers and the Phillies and the Cardinals and all that cheap s**t. All these motherf**kin' editorials about [inaudible] and f**kin', uh, the Phillie-itis and all that s**t. It's sickening. It's unbelievable. It really is. It's a disheartening f**kin' situation that we're in right now. Five and fourteen doesn't negate all that work. We got a hundred and forty-three f**kin' games left. What I'm trying to say is don't rip them f**kin' guys out there. Rip me. If you wanna rip somebody, rip my f**kin' ass. But don't rip them f**kin' guys 'cause they're givin' everything they can give. . . . But once we hit that f**kin' groove . . . it will flow. And it will flow—the talent's there. I don't know how to make it any clearer to you. I'm frustrated. I'll guarantee you I'm frustrated. It would be different if I walked into this room every day at eight-thirty and saw a bunch of guys that didn't give a s**t. They give a s**t and it's a tough National League East. It's a tough National League period."

Elia's rant is familiar to Wrigley Field regulars. What is not well known is what preceded it and probably triggered it.

In those days, when the Cubs left the playing field at the end of the game, they could not reach their clubhouse, as they now do, through their first-base dugout. Instead, they had to go under the grandstand through an entrance farther down the left-field line. The Cubs' right fielder that day was Keith Moreland, "a redheaded snapdragon"—his description—from Texas, where he had played defensive end for the University of Texas Longhorns football team. Defensive ends are not shrinking violets. In 2013, when he was the color analyst on Cubs radio broadcasts, he recalled that as he walked down the left-field line that day thirty years earlier, a fan—or at least a spectator—offered what might be considered negative feedback on the team's performance. The person, who had probably partaken too liberally of Heileman's Old Style lager, threw a cup of that beverage in Moreland's face, drenching him. Moreland had a football player's zest for combat and the sort of temper commonly ascribed to redheads. He headed into the stands after the beer thrower, but two strong hands grabbed the back of his belt to restrain him. One hand belonged to relief pitcher Lee Smith, a mountain of a man then in his fourth season with the Cubs, the first of eight teams he played for in eighteen seasons, during which he recorded 478 saves, the third most in baseball history. Smith stood six feet five and weighed at least 220 pounds. The other hand belonged to Elia, who kept up a steady flow of expletives as he and Smith propelled Moreland into the clubhouse. Moreland assumed the profanity was directed at him for charging into the stands and braced himself for a tongue lashing and perhaps a fine. It turned out, however, that Elia was just tuning up his voice and vocabulary for his philippic against Cub fans, who he thought lowered the tone of the Friendly Confines.

The "f**kin' groove," the "flow" that Elia anticipated, never quite arrived in 1983. The Cubs did, however, improve somewhat, finishing fifth, with a 71–91 record. Wrigley Field's lights were still five years away, so the customers who were the subject of Elia's disapproval, the 15 percent of the people in the world who had the time to come to day baseball, included all of the Cubs' customers. Elia was fired.

In 1984, one of the happier summers Wrigley Field has seen, Tobias J. Moskowitz and L. Jon Wertheim were not there. They were, in their own words, "a pair of sports-crazed twelve-year-olds from Indiana," and both were members of Bunk 7 at Camp Young Judaea in Ortonville, Michigan. Their resemblance to baseball Hall of Famers Hank Greenberg and Sandy Koufax began and ended with their being Jewish. But even at their young age, they brought to the camp's softball games an analytic intensity that might have had something to do with the fact that they were Cub fans. If you are (as they were) intelligent, observant, and curious, the experience of being a Cub fan leads to an itch to explain the seemingly inexplicable—the astonishing consistency of the Cubs' futility.

In 1984, the Cubs were thirty-nine years from their last World Series appearance, seventy-six years from their last World Series victory, and well into what has become the longest run without a championship of all North American professional sports franchises. In 2011, the two former campers collaborated in trying to explain this in their book *Scorecasting: The Hidden Influences Behind How Sports Are Played and Games Are Won.* Their last chapter is titled "Are the Chicago Cubs Cursed?" Its subtitle is: "If Not, Then Why Are the Cubs So Futile?" By now, you will not be surprised to learn that Moskowitz and Wertheim think that one reason is Wrigley Field.

They begin by rejecting a rival explanation: bad luck. No one, they say, thinks that it is by luck that the Yankees have won twenty-seven World Series. Or that the Cubs' principal rival, the Cardinals, have won the second-most World Series, eleven. Luck implies randomness, an outcome not commensurate with ability. Hence luck is, they rightly note, "inherently immeasurable."

If the Cubs were just unlucky in consistently not winning their division, they should at least have frequently finished second to the Cardinals in it. But Moskowitz and Wertheim note that the Cubs have finished second even

fewer times than they have finished first. They have finished third more times than either first or second, they have
finished fourth more times than third, and have finished
last seventeen times. This, Moskowitz and Wertheim say
with nice understatement, "is not consistent with luck."
Neither is the obverse: The Yankees have finished first
(much) more often than second; they have finished second
more often than third; they have finished third more often
than fourth; and they have finished last only three times.

If luck falls short as an explanation for either the success
or the failure of teams on the field, you would think that
the opposite of luck—talent—would provide the answer.
And you would be correct, say Moskowitz and Wertheim:

> Historically, for the average MLB team, its on-the-
> field statistics would predict its winning percent-
> age year to year with 93 percent accuracy. That
> is, if you were to look only at a team's on-the-field
> numbers each season and rank it based on those
> numbers, 93 percent of the time you would get
> the same ranking as you would if you ranked it
> based on wins and losses. . . . Based on this mea-
> sure, how unlucky are the Cubs? Did the Cubs
> lose more games than they should have based on
> their performance at the plate, on the mound,
> and in the field? Unfortunately (for us Cub fans),
> no. . . . The Cubs' ritual underperformance in
> terms of wins is perfectly understandable when
> you examine their performance on the field. To

put it more precisely, if we were to predict year to year the Cubs' winning percentage based on all available statistics, we would be able to explain 94 percent of it, which is slightly higher than the league average.

So the Cubs would seem to be, if anything, slightly *less* unlucky than the average MLB team. The unsurprising conclusion is that in this sport of the long season, in which 162 games reduce the role of randomness, a.k.a. luck, the Cubs' failures are explained by lack of talent. Hence the interesting question is why the Cubs' management has consistently put inferior teams on the field, which brings us to the concept central to all economic reasoning: incentives.

All professional sports teams have monetary reasons for wanting to excel. But some have weaker incentives than others. For almost all teams, the interests of the fans and of the owners are congruent. But, as we shall see, there are differences, especially for one team.

Fans want victories because winning is fun and fun is the point of being a fan. Owners want victories because they want fans to make the turnstiles spin and buy beers to wash down the hot dogs, and to listen to and watch the teams' broadcasts. So Moskowitz and Wertheim ask an obvious question: How is attendance at home games related to the home team's on-field success? This is their answer:

Calculating the response of home game attendance to season performance for every MLB team over the last century, we get a measure of how sensitive fans are to team success. If this number equals one, it means that when a team wins 10 percent more games, attendance rises by 10 percent—in other words, one for one. Greater than one means attendance rises by more than 10 percent (fans are more sensitive to performance), and less than one means fans are not as sensitive to performance, creating fewer incentives to win.

Do you see where this is heading?

Cubs attendance "is the least sensitive to performance in all of baseball." The Yankees' attendance sensitivity is 0.9, "meaning that attendance moves almost one for one with winning percentage." Red Sox attendance sensitivity also is 0.9, which must have *something* to do with why these two teams have done so much winning. The sensitivity of Cubs attendance per game to winning percentage is only 0.6, much less than one. "The league average is one," write Moskowitz and Wertheim. So "the Cubs are America's Teflon team," which must have *something* to do with why they have done so much losing.

Comparing Cubs and White Sox season attendance numbers from 1998 through 2009, Moskowitz and Wertheim found that Cubs attendance varied between 82 percent and 99 percent of Wrigley Field's capacity. White Sox attendance was 37 percent of their home field's capacity in 1999 and 90 percent of capacity in 2006, the year after the team won the World Series. In 2006, the Cubs finished last and averaged 94 percent of Wrigley Field's capacity. And the 165,801 more fans the Cubs drew into Wrigley than the White Sox attracted to U.S. Cellular Field do not include the many thousands of fans who purchased seats on the rooftops across from Wrigley on Waveland and Sheffield Avenues.

In the 2013 season, the one hundredth played at Wrigley Field, the home team did something never done in any of the previous ninety-nine: It lost fifty home games. The previous record was forty-nine, set in 1971. In 2013, Cubs attendance declined, as it has done in every season since 2008, when the Cubs won the National League Central and drew a franchise-record 3.3 million. But in 2013, even while setting a record for Friendly Confines futility, the team drew about seven hundred *more* fans per game than did the 1998 team that played in the postseason as winner of the National League wild card.

You can say this for Cub fans: They are not front-runners. You can say this against them: They are incorrigible. In 2002, the Cubs lost 13 percent more games than in 2001, but attendance *increased* 1 percent. Nothing new there. In 1999, the Cubs lost 14 percent more games than in 1998—and attendance increased 7 percent. Attendance rates at Wrigley are, write Moskowitz and Wertheim, "as steady as a surgeon's hands." But what is healthy in surgery is unhealthy in baseball.

In baseball, the difference between excellence and mediocrity is usually not the blockbuster signing of this or that free agent. Rather, it is the cumulative effect of management's attention to scouting, player development, and so on—which requires time, effort, and, always, money. Because Cub fans fill so many seats no matter what is happening on the field, there is a reduced incentive to pay the expense of organizational excellence.

It was in 1932 that *Harpers Magazine* quoted P. K. Wrigley on giving the fans a reason other than good baseball for going to the ballpark: "The fun . . . the sunshine, the relaxation. Our idea is to get the public to go see a ball game, win or lose." Again, there is a lot of losing in baseball, even for the best teams. If you can't bear losing, find another sport. And if you do not much mind losing, or if you actually rather enjoy it, you should feel right at home in Wrigley Field. With an acerbic terseness perhaps born of frustration, Moskowitz and Wertheim say, "There is equity in futility." That is, the Cubs may have had a perverse financial incentive to cultivate the image of "lovable losers." And speaking of incentives and, as any baseball person must, of beer, they also say, "Attendance at Wrigley Field is actually more sensitive to beer prices—much more—than it is to the Cubs' winning percentage."

Moskowitz and Wertheim studied Wrigley Field beer prices, adjusted for inflation, between 1984 and 2009 and concluded that attendance was *four times* more sensitive to beer prices than to the team's won-lost record. They do not make clear exactly how they come to that conclusion, but they do offer this tantalizing data: Over the two decades beginning in 1990, while the Cubs were compiling a 48.6 winning percentage, the team's management in-

creased ticket prices 67 percent, far above the MLB average of 44.7 percent. By 2009, Cubs ticket prices (average:
$48) were the third highest in all of baseball, behind only
those of the Red Sox, in the smallest major league park,
Fenway ($50), and the Yankees, in the ostentatious new
Yankee Stadium ($73). Demand for Cubs tickets remained
remarkably inelastic. But the team knew better than to
tamper with beer prices, which remained the third lowest
in the major leagues. "Only the small-market Pittsburgh
Pirates (at $4.75 a beer) and the medium-market Arizona
Diamondbacks (at $4.00) had cheaper beer—and their av-
erage ticket prices were $15.39 and $14.31, respectively."
"Cub fans," Moskowitz and Wertheim conclude, "will tol-
erate bad baseball *and* high ticket prices but draw the line
at bad baseball and expensive beer."

If you stand in the middle of the intersection of Clark and
Addison Streets and slowly turn in a circle, your gaze will
fall on a lot of places, including the ballpark, for drinking
beer. Of course, Wrigley Field, unlike the various bars
and restaurants and rooftops, is not *for* drinking beer. And
yet . . .

If you believe, as baseball fans are inclined to, that the
point of the Big Bang was to set in motion the process—the
universe, et cetera—that led to baseball, you should believe

that beer was part of the Plan from the start. Beer, it seems, has been crucial to the flourishing of civilization, and the connection between beer and baseball, two of civilization's better products, has been close and longstanding. Indeed, a case can be made that civilization is a result of, and flourished because of, beer.

For three million years, give or take a bunch, human beings went about the business of evolving from lower primates, and they did so without the assistance and comfort of alcohol. About one hundred thousand years ago they were more or less recognizably human, but they had not yet developed agriculture, so they had to keep moving around to find food. Then, according to the Discovery Channel program *How Beer Saved the World*, they began—by a happy accident, and even before mankind started baking bread— brewing beer. Humans were nomads, hunter-gatherers who occasionally gathered barley that was growing in the wild. One day, when some of these people were off on extended hunting-and-gathering treks, rain fell on barley they had stored in clay pots. The rain made the barley soggy, which was bad. But it also, with the help of natural sugars and other ingredients in the grain, and also airborne yeasts, started the process of fermentation, which was very good indeed. Eventually, homeward the hunters and gatherers made their weary way, and, being understandably thirsty from their exertions, they took a sip of the resulting fluid in the jars. Thus did humanity's era of sobriety come to an end.

One sip led to others, and to the desire for more beer,

which required more barley, which required systematic agriculture. So humanity vowed to put aside its nomadic ways, to develop the plow, and irrigation, and the wheel, so there could be carts to get surplus barley to markets. While they were at it, they developed writing to record commercial transactions, mathematics to make possible land sales and business computations, and, eventually, the U.S. Department of Agriculture and farm subsidies—all to keep the beer flowing.

An inscription on an ancient Egyptian tomb says that one thousand jugs of beer is about the right provision for the afterlife. The toiling masses who built the pyramids were paid in beer chits—a sort of early version of debit cards—and drank about a gallon of beer a day. It was what moderns disdainfully call near beer, only 3 percent alcohol. But it was nutritious enough to enable the toilers to pile up all that stone.

Beer was not only a stable food and a kind of currency, it was also a medicine. Traces of the antibiotic tetracycline, which was invented (or so we thought) in 1952, were found by puzzled archaeologists in the mummified bones of ancient Egyptians. Long before Alexander Fleming won the 1945 Nobel Prize for medicine as a result of his contribution to the development of penicillin, tetracycline was a health-enhancing residue of beer.

Beer also rescued the Middle Ages from a scourge and killer: water. Living centuries before the discovery of the germ theory of disease, people drank pond water fouled by human sewage, defecating ducks, waste from tanneries, butchers' offal, and other insalubrious ingredients. Brewing, however, removed many of the microorganisms that made people sick. It was, therefore, probably good that people then drank three hundred quarts of beer a year, which is six times today's consumption by American adults.

"The search for unpolluted drinking water is as old as civilization itself." So wrote Steven Johnson in *The Ghost Map: The Story of London's Most Terrifying Epidemic—and How It Changed Science, Cities, and the Modern World.* In his account of the cholera epidemic of 1854, Johnson explains that the beginning of civilization occurred with the formation of settled communities, and mass settlements also brought the beginnings of waterborne diseases, often from the settlements' human wastes, especially feces. "For much of human history," writes Johnson, "the solution to the chronic public-health issue was not purifying the water supply. The solution was to drink alcohol."

Alcohol has antibacterial properties that in early human settlements were more beneficial than the risks of alcohol were baneful. As Johnson says, "Dying of cirrhosis of the liver in your forties was better than dying of dysentery in your twenties." Alcohol is addictive and, consumed immoderately, is a potentially lethal poison. People who drink lots of it—who can "hold their liquor," as the saying goes—are apt to be those whose bodies, thanks to some genes on chromosome 4 in human DNA, are especially able to produce particular enzymes. Among the early agrarians who abandoned the hunter-gatherer lifestyle and dwelled together in settlements, those who lacked this genetic advantage were doomed by a Darwinian selection that favored those who could drink more. Here is Johnson on those who died young and childless, either from alcohol's ravages or from waterborne diseases:

> Over generations, the gene pool of the first farmers became increasingly dominated by individuals who could drink beer on a regular basis. Most of the world's population today is made up of descendants of those early beer drinkers, and we have largely inherited their genetic tolerance for alcohol.

Well. If beer is, strictly speaking, a health food, then Wrigley Field, which has been called the world's largest outdoor singles bar, is actually also a health club, of sorts.

It has been accurately said that the United States is the only nation founded on a good idea: the pursuit of happiness, of which baseball is an important ingredient. But there also is a sense in which America was founded on beer. Within two years of the 1607 founding of Jamestown, Virginia, leaders of that settlement wrote to London, asking that a brewer be sent out because "water drinkers"—the phrase drips disdain—were no basis for a colony. Which was true, but for reasons they could not have then known, not understanding about germs. The *Mayflower* put passengers ashore in what would become Massachusetts, although its captain had been searching for a landing much farther south; the problem, according to William

Bradford's journals, lay in "our victuals being much spent, especially beer." While Thomas Jefferson was brewing beer at Monticello, his boon companion James Madison diluted his limited government convictions enough to consider advocating the establishment of a national brewery to provide a wholesome alternative to whiskey. It almost seems that Manifest Destiny pointed toward Wrigleyville.

George Washington, Sam Adams, and Thomas Jefferson were among our Founding Brewers, and beer was integral to the Internet of colonial America—the communications network of taverns, such as the Green Dragon in Boston, where, on the evening of December 16, 1773, some patriots decided to go down to the docks and toss cases of tea into the harbor. When the nation was born, it needed a national anthem, and it found one by giving new words to what had been a drinking song that sometimes served as a sobriety test: If you could sing it, you could have another tankard of beer. In the 1860s, beer, not milk, became the first beverage to be pasteurized. The reason beer could spoil was that it was alive. It contained a hitherto unknown life-form, bacteria, which could make beer sick—and people, too. Hence the cornerstone of modern medicine, the previously mentioned germ theory.

What America needed was not just better medicine but more fun. Fun-loving Benjamin Franklin had understood this when he'd said, "Beer is living proof that God loves us and wants us to be happy." It was not, however, until the nineteenth century, when German immigrants began arriving in large numbers, that America had a cohort that took fun seriously. The German immigrants were astonished, and not happily, to find that there was no beer culture and, not coincidentally, no culture of pleasure. The German Americans set about rectifying this defect in the Republic by creating beer gardens where people could play cards to the accompaniment of music.

Most beer was drunk in taverns, some of which had basements where ice cut from northern lakes kept the beer cool in the summer. But ice was not always cheap or plentiful, either because of warm winters or because, during part of the nineteenth century, ice was, by weight, America's biggest export, sent as far as India and China. And American beer that was taken home from taverns in pails would last only a day before spoiling because of the absence of refrigeration.

It was the American preference for one particular form of beer—lager, which has to be brewed slowly and at cold temperatures—that led brewers to drive the development of refrigeration, which made possible a constant supply of beer year-round. It also solved mankind's problem of food storage and made Las Vegas possible.

Before the mechanics of refrigeration and the technique of pasteurization arrived from Europe, beer had been brewed in batches of seven to ten barrels a day. Now, suddenly, there were the technological prerequisites for the emergence of beer barons. Emerge they did, and some of their German names—such as Adolphus Busch, Gottlieb

Heileman, Frederick Pabst, Joseph Schlitz, and Bernhard Stroh—would eventually be emblazoned on the labels of billions of beer bottles and cans.

By the turn of the twentieth century, when the beer business was booming enough to finance advertising ("Budweiser gives punch to the lunch"), most beer was sold in "tied houses"—taverns tied to particular breweries. Soon there were many more taverns than could survive by simply selling beer. So they branched out, doing a brisk business in gambling and prostitution. This, in turn, fueled the Prohibition movement, which was so vividly embodied in Carry Nation, who, as Daniel Okrent writes in *Last Call: The Rise and Fall of Prohibition*, was "six feet tall, with the biceps of a stevedore, the face of a prison warden, and the persistence of a toothache." This hatchet-wielding scourge of taverns used a vigorous persuasion technique called "hatchetization."

On the defensive, brewers argued in vain that distilled spirits, not beer, were the real alcohol problem. Perhaps that was so, but during Prohibition, which arrived in January 1920, spirits fared better than beer because beer is bulky and therefore difficult to smuggle into the country or on your person. As support grew for repealing Prohibition, the Woman's Christian Temperance Union warned that "no nation ever drank itself out of a depression." To which the nation responded: Maybe not, but drink might make the Depression more endurable. Prohibition ended in 1933, but serious damage had been done: America had lost much of its taste for beer. Beer consumption did not reach pre-Prohibition quantities until the 1970s. Which was certainly not Wrigley Field's fault.

In the second half of the nineteenth century, baseball did much to help the nation shed some of its Puritan earnestness and learn to play, or to relax by watching others play. In the second half of the twentieth century, baseball helped the nation reacquire its thirst for beer. In 1950, Heileman's Old Style lager became not just the only beer then sold at Wrigley Field but the official beer of the place. Although Heileman is now owned by Pabst—these familiar names do endure—Heileman's association with the Cubs is older than Anheuser-Busch's with the St. Louis Cardinals, who today play in their third ballpark to bear the Busch name. Wrigley Field, like all ballparks but more than some, performs a function that taverns used to perform: It brings people out of their homes and together for a social drink. Home refrigerators helped prompt the shift of beer drinking from taverns to homes, and by the time Prohibition ended, one-third of all beer sold was not from a tap but in a bottle. By 1940, half was. By 1960, 80 percent was sold in bottles or cans. Today, millions of bottles and cans are emptied in the North Side tavern that also is a ballpark.

To the delight of fans who work while the sun shines, night games came to Major League Baseball on May 24, 1935, in

Cincinnati's Crosley Field. This was the handiwork of Larry MacPhail, grandfather of Andy MacPhail, who would be president of the Cubs through twelve seasons, 1994–2006. By the 1938 season, two of the fourteen ballparks (the St. Louis Cardinals and Browns shared Sportsman's Park, and the Philadelphia Phillies and Athletics shared Shibe Park) had lights. If the Cubs had had lights that year, the most dramatic home run ever hit by the home team would have been drained of much of its drama.

On September 28, 1938, the Cubs were half a game behind the first-place Pirates as the two teams continued a three-game series at Wrigley Field. Late in the afternoon of an overcast day, the game was tied 5–5 as the Cubs came to bat in the bottom of the ninth, and the home plate umpire announced that the game would be called at the end of the inning if the Cubs did not score. At 5:37 P.M., with two outs, no runners on base, and no one able to see much of anything, Gabby Hartnett hit a two-strike pitch for what would ever after be known as the "Homer in the Gloamin'." The next day the Cubs pummeled the Pirates 10–1, earning the right to be trounced by the Yankees in a four-game World Series in which they were outscored 22 to 9.

In 1936, when the two leagues had separate governance under their own presidents, the American League gave its members permission to have night games. Until 1942, each American League team was allowed to have only seven a season. This restriction was relaxed in 1942 to accommodate people working long hours in war industries. By 1948, when lights were installed in Briggs Stadium in Detroit, only Wrigley Field was without them. Soon the absence of lights became a symbol of a superior sensibility to some baseball "purists." Never mind that P. K. Wrigley had bought those materials for installing lights after the 1941 season but then had donated the steel to the war effort.

When, however, the Cubs got to the National League play-offs against the Padres in 1984, the introduction of lights to Wrigley Field became inevitable. Commissioner Peter Ueberroth knew that Major League Baseball's national broadcast partners, having paid steep fees in anticipation of prime-time audiences, would not accept daytime games. So Ueberroth said that in future seasons, any Cub postseason games might not be played at Wrigley Field. Four years later, on the evening of 8/8/88, the lights were switched on for the first night game at Wrigley, which was rained out in the third inning.

To the surprise of no one other than dismayed purists, most fans—impurists?—like night games. The dispensers of beers in Wrigleyville bars probably do not. They would prefer games to begin at, say, five P.M., so that fans leaving the ballpark around eight would not need to hurry home. Lights have, however, rendered anachronistic the portion of Lee Elia's rant about Cub fans being, necessarily, people who "don't even work."

Fourteen months later, Game 1 of the 1989 championship series between the Cubs and the San Francisco Giants was played in Wrigley Field and was broadcast by Vin Scully, who has been broadcasting Dodgers games (first Brooklyn, then Los Angeles) since 1950. Before the game, he waxed poetic about Wrigley Field:

> She stands alone at the corner of Clark and Addison, this dowager queen, dressed in basic black and pearls, seventy-five years old, proud head held high and not a hair out of place, awaiting yet another date with destiny, another time for Mr. Right. She dreams as old ladies will of men gone long ago. Joe Tinker. Johnny Evers. Frank Chance. And of those of recent vintage like her man Ernie. And the Lion [Leo Durocher]. And Sweet Billy Williams. And she thinks wistfully of what might have been, and the pain is still fresh and new, and her eyes fill, her lips tremble, and she shakes her head ever so slightly. And then she sighs, pulls her shawl tightly around her frail shoulders, and thinks, This time, this time it will be better.

Maybe. On the other hand, perhaps the old lady of the North Side is like Miss Havisham, the sad, spectral old woman in Charles Dickens's *Great Expectations*. She had found, or so she thought, Mr. Right in a swain named Compeyson. But at eight-forty A.M. on her wedding day, as she was dressing for the ceremony, she received a letter from him, revealing that he had defrauded her of her inheritance from her father, a successful brewer, and would not marry her. She responded by having all her clocks stopped at twenty minutes to nine. The table set for a banquet was left untouched, and she never changed out of her wedding dress. It eventually catches fire and she dies from the burns. This is Miss Havisham as seen through Pip's eyes:

> She was dressed in rich materials—satins, and lace, and silks—all of white. Her shoes were white. And she had a long white veil dependent from her hair, and she had bridal flowers in her hair, but her hair was white. . . . I saw that everything within my view which ought to be white, had been white long ago, and had lost its luster, and was faded and yellow. I saw that the bride within the bridal dress had withered like the dress, and like the flowers, and had no brightness left but the brightness of her sunken eyes. I saw that the dress had been put upon the rounded figure of a young woman, and that the figure on which it now hung loose, had shrunk to skin and bone.

So, no. Let us avoid thinking of Wrigley Field as a melancholy old lady. It—she—does, however, have one haunting memory of what might have been. It concerns an ugly episode that should be remembered whenever Cub fans get

misty-eyed and natter on about the "Friendly Confines."
Around ten P.M. on October 14, 2003, friendliness was suddenly in short supply at the corner of Clark and Addison.

The Cubs were leading the 2003 National League Championship Series against the Florida Marlins, as the Miami
Marlins were known then, three games to two. Ahead of
the Marlins 3–0 in the top of the eighth inning of Game
6, with a Marlins runner on second base, the Cubs were
five outs from their first World Series since 1945. For
Major League Baseball, that would be a matchup made
in heaven: David against Goliath, the Cubs against the
Yankees, perennial losers against the definition of the word
"dynasty." Then a Marlins batter lofted a soft fly ball down
the left-field line where the seats are only a few feet from
the foul line. Cubs left fielder Moises Alou, his glove hand
raised, crossed the foul line and reached for the ball. So did
some fans, including Steve Bartman.

A twenty-six-year-old computer consultant, a former
high school second baseman, a youth baseball coach, and
a besotted Cub fan, he was listening to the game through
headphones. He was sitting in aisle 4, row 8, seat 113, a
few feet from the wall. Except now, as the ball descended,
he was not sitting. He was doing what fans reflexively do:
standing and reaching for the ball, which was coming down

tantalizingly close to him. It was falling into the stands, not onto the field of play, which is why the umpires correctly ruled that what Bartman did was not fan interference. If he had reached out of the stands, he would have interfered with Alou, so the batter would have been out and the Cubs would have been four outs from the World Series. The relevant rule reads: "Spectator interference occurs when a spectator reaches out of the stands, or goes on the playing field, and touches a live ball." Bartman touched the ball. Alou, reaching into the stands, did not touch it. He made a gesture of angry frustration, slamming his fist into his glove, then trotted back to his position.

If Alou had not vented his frustration, the crowd probably would have turned its attention back to the game. But the gesture changed the crowd and Bartman's life. The crowd became a mob and Bartman became a pariah, and nearly a victim of violence. Neither team's manager questioned the umpire's call on the foul ball. I was sitting upstairs, behind home plate, with Cubs president Andy MacPhail. He glanced at a replay on a television in his box and murmured two words: "Good call." Then things turned ugly, on the field and even more so in the stands.

The Cubs unraveled. The Marlin batter, who had been given a second life when Alou didn't catch the foul ball, was walked. The next batter singled, driving in the runner on second. The following batter hit what certainly could have been, and probably should have been, a double-play grounder to the Cubs' shortstop, Alex Gonzalez. A fine defensive player, he led all National League shortstops in

fielding in 2003, and if he had fielded the grounder cleanly
the inning would probably have been over, leaving the
Cubs three outs from the World Series. But he bobbled it,
getting neither the runner at second nor the batter-runner
at first. The situation was now three men on, one out, and
bad karma rising.

The Cubs were still ahead 3–1. The game was proceed-
ing to a climax, but the attention of many in the ballpark
was focused not on the field but on the young man who,
it is important to remember, was just one person among
many who had reached for the descending foul ball. The
fan who'd plucked the ball from Wrigley's concrete floor
was not Bartman. But there were more than a dozen television cameras at this postseason game, and replays showed
that the hands that had deflected the ball away from Alou
belonged to the fellow wearing a green turtleneck and
headphones.

Catching Hell, ESPN's documentary on this event,
clearly records a spectator's voice saying, "Good job, asshole." Then another: "Somebody hit that cocksucker! Hit
him!" In the Marlins' dugout, third baseman Mike Lowell
remembers a teammate saying about Bartman, "Let's make
him famous, you know, make this a turning point." In a
few moments the score was 3–3. But instead of exhorting
the Cubs to stop the bleeding, much of the crowd, including the large throng gathered on Waveland Avenue outside
the left-field bleachers, was chanting, "Asshole! Asshole!
Asshole!" Then the chant turned to "Fuck you! Fuck you!"

Soon beer was being thrown on Bartman, and pizza

and pretzels. Before the third out of the disastrous eighth inning was recorded, the Marlins led, 8–3. That was the final score. The crowd continued to scream and throw debris at Bartman as security guards struggled to get him to safety. A famous fan said to a reporter, "If someone ever convicts that guy of a crime, he'll never get a pardon out of this governor." This was Rod Blagojevich, who eight years later was convicted of corruption and sentenced to fourteen years in prison.

Security personnel removed Bartman's glasses, headphones, and Cubs hat and dressed him in the white jacket worn by Wrigley Field safety services. Nevertheless, a fan outside the ballpark recognized Bartman, so a security officer who lived in the neighborhood took Bartman to her home. Later he was put in a van and driven to the hotel where he and two friends, who had been seated with him in the ballpark, had rented a room for their planned celebration of the victory that sent the Cubs to the World Series.

The next day, the *Chicago Sun-Times* published Bartman's name, the fact that he lived with his parents in the town of Northbrook, and the place where he worked. He released a statement apologizing "from the bottom of this Cub fan's broken heart." As far as is known, he has never returned to Wrigley Field.

If the next night the Cubs had won Game 7, Bartman would be a mere footnote in baseball history—the answer to a trivia question. But the Marlins scored three runs in the first inning of that game. The Cubs regained the lead after Alex Gonzalez doubled off the center-field wall and pitcher Kerry Wood drove him in with a home run. Moises Alou also hit a two-run home run. But the Cubs lost, 9–6.

The fan who scooped up the ball that blighted Bartman's life sold it in 2003 for $106,600. It was destroyed in a ceremony at Harry Caray's restaurant. Bartman was offered serious money—hundreds of thousands of dollars—to appear in commercials or make public appearances, but he never took a dime or any other benefit in exchange for telling his story.

Near the conclusion of *Catching Hell*, the narrator says, "As time passes, the city is haunted more by what it did to Bartman than what Bartman did to Chicago. There are many who say the city should forgive Bartman, but it's really up to Bartman to forgive Chicago." A former major leaguer who had some fine years with the Cubs spoke some sympathetic words for Bartman: "To get crucified the way he did was mind-boggling. He didn't do anything, he didn't do anything different. You take a major league baseball player and sat him in that seat, he'd have done the same thing that Bartman did. I mean I would have done it." So said Bill Buckner.

As I slowly inched my way down a congested Wrigley Field ramp after the final out of the Bartman game, a fan recognized me and shouted, "We'll get them tomorrow night, Mr. Will!" I replied, "Not a chance!" I had seen this movie before.

In 1984, the Cubs had advanced to the postseason for the first time since 1945. There were just two divisions in each league in 1984, and the division winners faced each other in a best-of-five play-off to determine who would meet in the World Series. The Cubs played the Padres. The first two games were in Wrigley Field, and the Cubs won both. As I left the park after the second game, with the Cubs heading to San Diego and needing to win just one game, I was walking next to Don Drysdale, the Dodgers' Hall of Fame pitcher who had been one of the broadcasters for the national telecast that day. He said to me, "Now, Will, do you Cub fans believe?" I said to him, "Every Cub fan knows it will be the Padres in five." The Cubs lost all three games in San Diego. They lost the last one because an unchallenging ground ball went through the legs of Cubs first baseman Leon Durham. This was two years before, in Game 6 of the Mets–Red Sox World Series, the Red Sox lost a chance to win their first World Series since 1918 because a softly hit ground ball went through the legs of former Cubs first baseman Bill Buckner.

In *Chicago: City on the Make*, Nelson Algren perfected the city's tough-guy tone of voice. The place "isn't so much a city as it is a vasty way station where three and a half million bipeds swarm." Yes, but. "Yet once you come to be part of this particular patch, you'll never love another. Like loving a woman with a broken nose, you may find lovelier lovelies. But never a lovely so real." Wrigley Field's loveliness is a function of how real it is, of its practicality.

Here, however, is an unlovely thought: Perhaps Wrigley Field should be decorated with a large warning akin to those that appear on packages of, and advertisements for, cigarettes. If the government were really *comprehensively* concerned with our potentially injurious choices, the big red sign that looms over Wrigley Field's home plate gates would read, "The Surgeon General has determined that this is a gateway to neurological difficulties." So say the contributors to a naughty book published in 2008, *Your Brain on Cubs: Inside the Heads of Players and Fans*. It is a collection of essays by doctors and others knowledgeable about neuroscience and brain disorders associated with giving one's allegiance to a team that last won a World Series exactly one hundred years before the book was published.

In a *New Yorker* cartoon depicting a man and a woman seated on a restaurant banquette, the man says, "OK, Cynthia, I'll tell you my hopes and dreams, my joys and my passions. But be forewarned—they all concern a particular sports team." The sometimes terrible truth is that being a sports fan is a physical phenomenon as well as a psychological condition. Without dogpaddling too far out into the deep philosophic water of the mind-body distinction, let us just say this: The world is divided between the many persons who say, "I have a body," and the few who say, "I am a body." I think that the more science teaches about the brain, the more reasons we have for thinking that the few speak correctly. They are supported by what neuroscience knows about being a sports fan, which involves observable—thanks to brain-imaging technology—alterations of brain matter.

Group memberships—in families, tribes, neighborhoods, cities, nations, religions—are common and powerful as components of identities. They are so common and powerful that they must be in some sense natural. We seem to be hardwired for such allegiances. Presumably they are adaptive aspects of the evolution of human beings as social creatures. But how does the group identity of Cub fans help them flourish? By giving them brain calisthenics.

This is the good news, and there is precious little of it in *Your Brain on Cubs*. It seems that "given the complex situations and thinking that Cub fans have had to engage in," their "frontal lobes are consistently activated" as they consider their thought-provoking affiliation. So says Jordan Grafman, a senior investigator at the National Institute of Neurological Disorders and Stroke, in suburban Washington, D.C. His thesis is the fruit of scientific education leavened by hard experience. He was born and raised in Chicago, so he knows whereof he speaks when he speaks, as he does delicately, about the "paradox" of being a Cub fan even though baseball is supposed to provide *relief* from life's problems. Grafman has been to the most pleasant of purgatories, Wrigley Field, and he has returned with good news.

Yes, rooting for the Cubs is a minority taste. How could it be otherwise? It is, after all, a lifelong tutorial in deferred gratification. But, Grafman says, "there is some evidence that being in the majority (everyone loves a winner) reduces reflective thinking." Rooting for a steady, consistent loser makes one thoughtful. Or perhaps neurotic. Which, on Chicago's North Side, may be a distinction without a difference. "The scientific literature," Grafman writes, "suggests that fans of losing teams turn out to be better decision-makers and deal better with divergent thought, as opposed to the unreflective fans of winning teams."

Relative to the brains of other animals, human brains have disproportionately large prefrontal cortexes. Hence the human knack for planning, reasoning, and experiencing subtle variations of feelings. Grafman tells us that when a fan's team wins, "the brain's reward system, including the ventral brain stem and basil ganglia," pumps dopamine into the brain, which gives—or perhaps *is*—the experience of intense pleasure. Narcotics do that, too. So, are fans of winning teams in danger of addiction? Perhaps. If so, are Cub fans fortunate because of their misfortune? No.

Kelli Whitlock Burton, a science writer, and Hillary R. Rodman, an associate professor of psychology at Emory University, cite studies of activities in the portion of the brain that registers depression, sadness, grief, and euphoria, the first three of which are pertinent to Wrigley Field patrons. Burton and Rodman note that drug addiction can cause changes in neural sensitivity and structure, and they wonder whether a Cub fan "has subtle and long-lasting changes in his or her brain reward circuitry, comparable to a kind of addiction." They also say that the "limbic structure called the amygdala, deep within the temporal lobe,

shows abnormally high activity in depressed patients."
Studies of "induced sadness"—for example, the brain activity of a person grieving about the end of a romantic
relationship—might tell us something about a brain on
Cubs. Furthermore, when rats are made to experience
"acute and persistent defeat," there are observable physi-
ological effects: Certain nerve cells undergo long-lasting
changes in their ability to respond electrically to stimuli.

Burton and Rodman report that scientists are identify-
ing "the chemical bases of long-lasting brain changes after
social defeat, with the neurotransmitter serotonin, which
is also heavily implicated in clinical depression, among
the substances most clearly involved." In sports fans, as
in players, a team's success or failure can cause hormonal
changes, particularly in the production of testosterone.
One implication of this might be that Cub fans, in a kind of
Darwinian natural de-selection, have trouble reproducing.

Two other contributors to *Your Brain on Cubs*, Tom
Valeo and Lindsay Beyerstein, say that cognitive neuroscience has found evidence that the brain strains to produce
explanations for things "and it will make up stories to cope
with phenomena it otherwise cannot account for." This
may indicate that we are hardwired for religion, which
generally explains as well as consoles and enjoins. And
the deep craving for explanations may explain why baseball is rich with superstitions, such as that of Julio Gotay,
a journeyman player for the Cardinals and others in the
1960s, who always took the field with a talismanic cheese
sandwich in his back pocket. Superstitions give people a

sense of security and control amid uncertainties. The brain "wants" to see outcomes as connected to preceding events. So fans get the brain-driven, if utterly irrational, pleasure of thinking that their rooting, which is a kind of prayer in a secular setting, somehow helps cause their teams' successes. It is said that there are no atheists in foxholes. There should be lots of them in Wrigley Field.

The science of economics has developed—and, say some economists, refuted—the efficient market hypothesis, which holds that it is impossible to consistently beat the securities market. The theory is that information travels quickly, and hence it is rapidly assimilated and incorporated into the price of stocks. The assumption, more elegant in theory than descriptive of reality, is that the prices of stocks generally reflect all the information that is available about them. Hence markets cannot be beaten, because they are "informationally efficient"; every participant knows as much as all other participants. Therefore over time, and not very much time, no stock or financial security trades significantly too cheaply or too expensively.

What has the efficient market hypothesis to do with the team that calls Wrigley Field home? Just this: The Cubs have done what should be almost impossible.

The efficient market hypothesis holds that no one, or

at any rate no one who is paying attention and is diligently trying to maximize his income, should be consistently beaten by the market. Applied by analogy to baseball, the efficient market hypothesis would hold that information about best practices, if available and understandable to all participants in the baseball "market," should produce a tendency toward equality in the competition for wins. Improvements in the conduct of the baseball business should become apparent to, and quickly adopted by, everyone paying attention.

We have seen this happen in recent decades regarding the "moneyball" practices. Consider the metrics by which Billy Beane's small-market Oakland Athletics found underpriced talent. To oversimplify radically, Beane looked for players whose high on-base percentages made them parsimonious with baseball's most precious commodities: outs. You are not beaten until you have made at least twenty-seven of them. So a team composed of players with high on-base percentages will be diligent about not beating itself. Beane's practices were observed and emulated even before the movie *Moneyball* made a drama out of a book that was as much a business treatise as a sports story. It was about how to price assets.

What successful teams do, they do in public. They do it under the intense, unblinking scrutiny of competitors, fans, and baseball journalists. Furthermore, teams operate within Major League Baseball's structure, which is designed to encourage competitive balance. Teams are regulated by a complex and always evolving collective bargaining agreement with the Major League Baseball Players Association, the union. Given these facts, you would think there would be no secrets, or none that remain secret for very long. Therefore, you would assume that under the efficient market hypothesis, as applied to success in baseball, which is measured in wins, no team could consistently "beat the market" by always winning—or losing. This is the assumption, even allowing for the differences in teams' resources that are permitted by Major League Baseball's economic model.

Under this model, there are substantial disparities in income deriving from intractable advantages and disadvantages associated with local broadcast revenues. No matter how intelligently the Pittsburgh Pirates and Kansas City Royals acquire and act on baseball's constantly evolving and enlarging fund of information, those two teams have relatively few television viewers in their areas and thus can buy fewer baseball assets than the Yankees, Dodgers, and other teams with gobs of money to put behind their use of universally available information. But even adjusting for such advantages, *similarly situated* teams should, over time, have similar results, meaning: No team should consistently beat the market, or the portion of the market competition most similar to it. And—you were wondering how this pertains to the Cubs?—no team should be consistently beaten, year after year, by similarly situated teams. But the Cubs are. The metric by which the team's management, for many decades, chose to measure success was fan contentment, disconnected from success on the field.

So on the North Side, the efficient market hypothesis was superseded by the Wrigley Field effect.

For several millennia—from the beginning of architecture until the second half of the nineteenth century—the height of buildings was limited by the load-bearing strength of stone. That is why Paris, London, Rome, and other old cities look as they do. Arguably, the first skyscraper was Chicago's ten-story Home Insurance Building, completed in 1885. Tall buildings were the result of a fortuitous congruence of two technologies and, in Chicago, an opportunity. The technologies were structural steel and the elevator. The opportunity was the open space provided by the great Chicago fire of 1871. The creation and evolution of Wrigley Field, however, involved no new technologies or material. Rather, it was born to be utilitarian, in the service of fun and games. It has not only survived but has become revered and emulated because it is so old it seems new.

Architectural antiquities are hard to come by in a nation whose largest city in 1776, Philadelphia, had a population of probably less than thirty thousand—smaller than a Wrigley Field sellout. Still, the phrase "American architectural antiquity" fits Wrigley Field, which is older than Manhattan's two most iconic skyscrapers, the Chrysler Building (1930) and the Empire State Building (1931). Wrigley is older than the glistening white temple of American law, the U.S. Supreme Court Building (1935). Wrigley is older than the Lincoln (1922) and Jefferson (1943) Memorials. It is older than the Hoover Dam (1936), the Golden Gate Bridge (1937), and the heads of the four presidents carved on Mount Rushmore, which were completed in 1941. As Wrigley Field turns one hundred, two years after Boston's Fenway Park reached that age, the average age of the other twenty-eight ballparks is about seventeen years.

Wrigley Field exemplifies something Winston Churchill understood. On May 10, 1941, a German air raid on London badly damaged the House of Commons, which moved its sessions to the House of Lords, in another part of the Palace of Westminster, on the bank of the Thames. On October 23, 1943, Prime Minister Churchill delivered a brief but lapidary speech concerning reconstruction of the Commons. "We shape our buildings," he said, "and afterward our buildings shape us." For that reason, he added, the House "should not be big enough to contain all its Members at once without overcrowding," and "there should be no question of every Member having a separate seat reserved for him." In a House of Commons large enough to accommodate everyone, most debates would be conducted in the depressing atmosphere of an almost-empty chamber. (As any viewer of C-SPAN knows, this is the case in both the House of Representatives and the Senate most of the time when the House and Senate are in session.) But, said Churchill, good parliamentary dialogue—quick, informal, conversational—"requires a fairly small space, and there should be on great occasions a sense of crowd and urgency." Besides, vitality of the House of Commons, and its hold on the nation's imagination, "depend to no small extent upon its episodes and great moments, even upon its scenes and rows, which, as everyone will agree, are better conducted at close quarters."

A good baseball park should reflect a comparable sensitivity to the relationship between space and usage. It was, after all, a great Chicago architect, Louis Sullivan, who said that "form ever follows function," and this axiom explains the beauty of old clipper ships and old baseball parks. Two other relevant axioms are self-evidently true, meaning they are accepted by all minds not clouded by cheerfulness. They are: Most new ideas are bad. And most improvements make matters worse. Both axioms were validated by the construction, in the 1960s and 1970s, of "dual-purpose" stadiums, used for both baseball and football. They were, of course, satisfactory for neither. This failure was predictable because—really, this is not complicated—the two sports' playing fields have different shapes.

Wrigley Field is primarily, and now exclusively (not counting concerts and other occasional uses and abuses), a baseball venue. For many years, however, it was the home field for Chicago Bears football games. Even as Wrigley Field turns one hundred, and even though the last NFL game was played there in 1970, it has still hosted the second-largest number of regular-season NFL games—365 of them. Only Giants Stadium, in northern New Jersey, which opened in 1976, was the site of more (495 through

2010), and only because it was also the home field for the New York Jets.

In the days before football succumbed to unlimited substitutions in the service of the modern mania for specialization, Bronko Nagurski played fullback on offense and tackle on defense for the University of Minnesota, from 1927 through 1929. In his senior season he became the first and last player to be named an all-American at two positions. From 1930 through 1937, he played for the Bears, who won NFL championships in 1932 and 1933. When the Second World War siphoned away many players, he came back for the 1943 season and the Bears won another championship. About six feet, two inches and 230 pounds, he would have been a normal-sized running back today. In his day, however, he was enormous. A much-told and perhaps even true story is that in a game in the close confinement of Wrigley Field, he galloped through assorted Washington Redskins and was not stopped until he crashed into the brick outfield wall. Returning to the huddle prior to the extra-point try, he said, "That last guy hit me awfully hard."

There. That is the last that shall be said here about football.

After people who probably liked neither baseball nor football were finished with the folly of dual-purpose stadiums— only the "coliseum" in Oakland remains in baseball—there was a merciful pause. Then something happened that we are constantly being told cannot happen: Someone turned the clock back.

The three most important things that have happened in baseball since the Second World War were Jackie Robinson taking the field in Brooklyn in 1947, free agency arriving in 1975, and Oriole Park at Camden Yards opening in 1992. This last was an act of heroic nostalgia but, then, baseball fans are disposed to live with cricks in their necks from looking backward. Which is why Major League Baseball owes a debt to a willowy woman from Mississippi. To those who said, "You can't turn back the clock," Janet Marie Smith responded, "Well, we'll just see about that."

Mississippi State University in Starkville has sent to the major leagues many baseball players, the greatest of whom was Will "the Thrill" Clark, the brash and talented hitter who, when he was playing in San Francisco, had a musical message on his telephone answering machine that announced, "The Thrill is gone." But Mississippi State's greatest gift to baseball has been the woman who understood how baseball could put more thrills in fans' experiences by learning from its oldest ballparks.

Born in 1957 in Jackson, Mississippi, she went to Starkville, where serendipity reared its lovely head. The School of Architecture, in which she enrolled, was then at the edge of campus, as was the baseball field. Aspiring architects and ballplayers mingled, and Smith began to acquire the baseball habit. After graduating with an architecture degree, she lived primarily in New York City from 1979 through 1984, working on Manhattan's Battery Park City and, in her spare time, earning a City College master's degree in urban design. During these years she took herself out to ball games at Yankee and Shea Stadiums, where she found in the crowds some respite from the anonymity of city life. Her next destination was Los Angeles. "I did not love the city but I did love Dodger baseball," she says. Dodger Stadium was, she notes, a rare public space in a famously dispersed city where she could experience the "energy" of concentrated people.

Eager to move back east and to find a project there, she visited Philadelphia, then Baltimore—the city she had picked when she was assigned, at City College, the task of dissecting a city's urban design opportunities. One day she found herself at an Orioles game in old Memorial Stadium, where a fan talked to her about rumored plans to build a new ballpark downtown as part of the Inner Harbor redevelopment. It would be the first time since the Fenway Park–Wrigley Field era that a baseball-only venue would be built in a city's downtown. The Oriole official driving this project was Larry Lucchino, who grew up in Pittsburgh before Forbes Field was replaced by the dual-purpose Three Rivers Stadium, which the Pirates shared with the NFL's Steelers for thirty years. Lucchino hired Smith, and together they fended off the idea of tearing down the nineteenth-century brick warehouse—one thousand feet long and fifty feet wide—that extends along the outfield and is a signature of Camden Yards' urban setting.

Wrigley Field was one of the places she, Lucchino, and others visited as they planned Camden Yards, and she came away from Chicago eager to build Camden Yards using

steel trusses of the sort that feature in Wrigley Field (and
Fenway Park), because they would distance Baltimore's
gem from the slab-of-concrete style of multipurpose ven-
ues. She especially liked how Wrigley's restrictions on in-
park advertising "allow you to soak in the green." She also
thought the rooftop seats across Waveland and Sheffield
added to the "social experience." Those seats were echoes
of the days, long ago, when fans outside many ballparks
stole glimpses of games by climbing lampposts or peering
through knotholes in fence planks.

Since participating in the creation of Camden Yards,
Smith has worked on Atlanta's Turner Field, Fenway
Park, and Dodger Stadium, helping to design the special
eating, drinking, and socializing places that ballparks seem
to require because, Smith says, "Americans today cannot
sit still for two and a half hours." (For today's games, they
would have to sit for almost three hours.) Wrigley Field,
which, fortunately, has scant space for such fripperies, requires fans to consider the game sufficient for their happiness.

Twenty major league parks have opened since Camden
Yards did, sixteen of them in downtown settings. Those sixteen have changed how people use cities. And the cities, by
forcing the ballparks to conform to the urban context, have
changed how the game is played, for this reason: Baseball
is the only sport that does not specify the dimensions of the
playing area, leaving latitude for different sizes and shapes
of outfields. So, Smith says, when a ballpark is built in an

existing urban neighborhood, the city is the tenth player on the field. This is notably so in the new ballpark most influenced by Wrigley Field.

In 2000, when AT&T Park, as it is now named, was new, San Francisco's then mayor, the amiable rapscallion Willie Brown, said the park felt as if it had been there for a couple of decades. Which is exactly what Larry Baer had in mind when he and his colleagues set out to replicate the feel of Wrigley Field as a neighborhood institution. Baer, president and chief executive officer of the extraordinarily successful Giants franchise, was present at the creation of the team's jewel of a ballpark. One of his challenges was to convince the neighborhood that bringing forty thousand or so people into it eighty-one times over six months would actually be pleasant. He says "the best $50,000 we spent" was for a model of the park and the neighborhood. He carted this around to meetings to assuage anxieties and even whet appetites for the pleasures of congestion caused by hordes of cheerful people. Baer was explicitly selling the idea of Wrigleyville West, and the neighborhood bought it.

The Giants shoehorned the ballpark into just 12.5 acres, hard by the bay in the city's China Basin section. This is the smallest patch of land for a new ballpark since Wrigley Field was built. None of the ballparks built since the Second World War occupy less than 35 acres, counting the space for parking. Some occupy 65 or 70 acres.

The small space dictated what the Giants wanted: an interestingly asymmetrical playing field. They particularly wanted right field to be so close to the water that long home runs would splash into it, landing among kayakers seeking souvenirs. Major League Baseball officials did not like the idea of a right-field foul line just 309 feet long. They thought cheap home runs would make a mockery of the game. But the Giants knew that few home runs—at least, few since their left-handed Hall of Famer Willie McCovey retired, in 1980—are pulled directly down the line. Besides, the right-field wall is 25 feet high. And to get over it, balls have to be driven through the thick ocean air. Furthermore, the outfield quickly deepens to 421 feet in right-center field. As a result, fewer home runs are hit to right field in AT&T Park than in any other major league park. And the Giants build their teams to fit their ballpark, collecting hitters who drive the ball into the deep left-center-field and right-center-field gaps for doubles and triples. Thus an exciting offense was made necessary by a ballpark configuration that itself was made necessary by the small footprint available to it.

If you are going to plunk a ballpark down smack-dab in the middle of a mature city, you are not going to have significant space for parking, but the Giants were right to not fret about this. The day the ballpark opened, Baer counted eight transportation modes—besides private cars, which did not bring even a plurality of fans—that fans used to get to the game. They walked, took taxis or buses or light rail or commuter rail, rode boats (from the East Bay) or bikes, or skated on Rollerblades.

Fans coming to Wrigley Field have the usual urban transportation options, but the most important is the El, the network of elevated trains that disgorge fans at Wrigley's right-field corner. Getting there really is part of the fun. The song says, "Take me out to the ball game, take me out with the crowd." Being *with* the crowd is, in and of itself, exciting because it is immersion in a temporary but regularly reconstituted cohort of the like-minded and high-spirited. This cohort acquires much of its mass before the game, from mass transit. The congestion of the El's cars compacts people into a kind of organism.

The venue is more important in baseball than in any other sport, for two reasons. The first is that baseball, with nine defensive players thinly dispersed across an eye-pleasing swath of green grass and reddish-tan manicured dirt, is best seen in person rather than on television. Clark Griffith is a Minneapolis lawyer and a grandson of the Clark Griffith who owned the Washington Senators a century ago. His grandfather was the wit who said, "Fans like home runs and we have assembled a pitching staff to please our fans." The grandson notes that a baseball field is larger than any other field in team sports not involving animals, meaning it is smaller than a polo pitch.

Second, because baseball is a game of discrete episodes rather than of flow, like basketball or soccer or hockey, baseball allows contemplation and conversation and a

general awareness of where you are. Or at least it allows it
when baseball owners do not take leave of their senses and
try to replicate, with loud music, the excruciating experience of being in an NBA arena. The NBA experience—
strobe lights, lasers, smoke, and cacophonous music—is
like being held prisoner in a Wurlitzer jukebox. The preva-
lent music at Wrigley is supplied by an organ. This instru-
ment provided the only sound at movies when they were a
rival entertainment during the first decade or so of Wrigley's existence. The Cubs became the first major league
team with an organ when they installed theirs at Wrigley in
1941. It is still all the sound track a game needs.

William Zinsser, a gifted writer of short essays, is a New
Yorker who gloomily anticipated the coming of the new
Yankee Stadium and the Mets' new Citi Field because he
assumed that they would "feature the latest advances in
audio-visual assault." He said he had quit going to Mets
games when the din made it impossible for him to talk
with whomever he was with. Baseball, he wrote, has its dis-
tinctive sounds but it is also "a game of silences. Every half
inning it invites its parishioners to meditate on what they
have just seen and to recall other players they once saw
play." This is why he thought "memory was the glue that
held baseball together as the continuing American epic."
And that is why music, other than that supplied by Wrigley
Field's organ, dissolves the glue.

This also means that Cubs hitters do not have "walk-
up" music—songs, or snippets of them, that are played
each time a batter approaches the plate. The Cubs experi-

mented with this, and the players liked it, but the Wrigley Field sound system was too primitive to make it a success. On the North Side, primitivism has served civilization, so far. At a baseball park, the loudest noise should be supplied by the spectators.

For twelve seasons, mostly with the Brooklyn Dodgers, Ralph Branca was a successful right-handed pitcher with a career record of eighty-eight wins and sixty-eight losses, including a twenty-one-win season in 1947. He is, however, remembered for one pitch. Bobby Thomson of the New York Giants hit it over the head of a former Wrigley Field favorite—Andy Pafko, a member of the 1945 Cubs' World Series team—and into the Polo Grounds' left-field stands to win the 1951 pennant. Branca should, however, also be known for his bittersweet 2011 memoir, *A Moment in Time: An American Story of Baseball, Heartbreak, and Grace*. In it he recalls the pleasure of playing major league baseball in a normal city neighborhood:

> Walking through Flatbush, you came upon Ebbets Field like you'd come upon a local candy store, a Jewish deli, or an Italian grocery. Ebbets Field was in and of itself a local character—

unassuming and unpretentious. Yankee Stadium
was and is monumental. The Polo Grounds was
bizarrely sculpted, with an endless center field
and imposing overhanging stands. Ebbets Field
wasn't bizarre. It was comforting and ordinary.
It was a happy resident in a residential neighborhood.

For a century, Wrigley Field has been like that. As it
enters its second century, however, the residential neighborhood is, if not unhappy, certainly uneasy, and those
who love the ballpark worry that its unassuming character
might perish.

On April 14, 2013, the Cubs' management announced
an agreement whereby the city would permit the team to
proceed with $500 million worth of improvements to the
ballpark and its immediate environs. Earlier that day, the
Cubs had lost to the San Francisco Giants. The Cubs had
blown a lead; the go-ahead run had scored on a balk; and
Cubs pitchers had tied a major league record by throwing five wild pitches in an inning, which at least distracted
attention from the four walks they surrendered in that
inning. Some incorrigible skeptics said that the most important part of the agreement was that the Cubs hence-
forth would be allowed to sell beer for an extra half inning,
through the end of the seventh, which would enable future
fans to be feeling no pain when the late innings were disappointing. But perhaps there will be many more games

at Wrigley Field when fans will be delighted because, the home team being ahead, they will not get to see the bottom of the ninth inning.

The Wrigley family's connection with the Cubs ended in 1981, when the team was bought for $205 million by the Tribune Company, which owns the *Chicago Tribune* newspaper, among other things. The other things included WGN, a "superstation" available throughout the nation that needed programming. The Cubs were attractive for this purpose, particularly because television has never been fastidious about filling time with excellence. Even when the team was unsuccessful on the field, it was a rollicking success at filling three or more hours of WGN's time. Ratings varied somewhat with success on the field, however. In 2007, the Tribune Company was bought by Sam Zell, who inexplicably thought that would be a good time to go into the newspaper business. It wasn't, but Zell's peculiar decision marked him as born to own the Cubs. When his empire came unglued, the Cubs were for sale.

Since 2008, for the first time since William Wrigley died, in 1932, the Cubs have had ownership as serious as baseball has become as a business. The Ricketts family of Omaha continues to run Ameritrade, the online broker business founded by Joseph Ricketts, who built the family

fortune. But today Tom Ricketts, one of Joseph's four children, runs the team. He has some other financial interests,
but Cubs baseball is his vocation, in the original meaning
of that word: It is his calling.

For one summer, Tom lived over a bar—the Sports Corner Bar, which is still there, in a new iteration—at the corner of Sheffield and Addison. He met his wife in Wrigley
Field's center-field bleachers. He was sitting with his father
on one of the rooftops across the street when he convinced
his father that buying the Cubs would be a good idea. He
said owning the team would be like owning "a 50-year
zero-coupon bond."

To put that in plain English for those of us who are
not conversant with the complexities of financial instru-
ments: Like such a bond, the Cubs will become more
valuable over time. The old rule, which is not quite true
but is true enough, is that you do not make money getting into baseball; you make money getting out. That is,
the value of a franchise grows over time. That will remain
true, if the future is like the past, which it generally is until
the moment when it isn't. The Tribune Company bought
the Cubs from the William Wrigley Jr. Company for $20.5
million in 1981. In 2009, the Ricketts family paid the Tribune Company $845 million for the team.

Fortunately, it has become more feasible to make
money by being in baseball. This is so for various reasons.
One is the increased revenue sharing among the teams.
Another is the explosive growth of television rights fees because technology now enables viewers to tape the program-

ming they like and watch it when they like, fast-forwarding through commercials—but they cannot do that with live sports. One of television's purposes is to sell beer and pickup trucks to young men, who are (in televisionspeak) a "coveted demographic" for sports broadcasting.

So, Joe Ricketts was convinced by son Tom, and the family acquired a franchise with a troubled history. It also bought a ballpark that is Illinois's third-most-popular tourist attraction, after Chicago's Navy Pier and the city's Museum Campus, which includes the Field Museum of Natural History, the Shedd Aquarium, and the Adler Planetarium. The team the family bought was not in good shape, and neither was Wrigley Field. The problems with the former were many and were written in numbers: The Cubs were thirty-six games under .500 through the first three years (2010–2012) the Ricketts owned them. Wrigley Field had three problems. First, large and potentially lethal bits of it would be falling on fans' heads were it not for nets rigged to catch the crumbling concrete. Second, the ballpark was not configured for modern players' needs, from batting cages to video of their at bats in the game under way. Third, the ballpark had to be operated under commercial and political restrictions that limited its ability to generate revenues sufficient to make the Cubs competitive. The restrictions included limits on advertising signs and on the number of night games. The latter limits are partly to assuage the anxieties of Wrigleyville residents, and partly to please the bar owners who have communicated to the local alderman their desire to limit the nights when fans do all their beer drinking inside Wrigley Field.

To Cub sentimentalists—and they are too numerous for the team's own good—it probably seems tacky to talk about making Wrigley Field more efficient at generating money. To them, this is akin to discussing how to sell the naming rights to Chartres. But what the Cubs do is play *professional* baseball. So, sentimentalists: Get over it.

During its ninety-ninth year, Wrigley Field sometimes generated more news for the business pages than for the sports pages. The issue was refurbishment, not just to remove those unsightly and disconcerting nets but also to allow the Cubs to maximize revenues. A major bone of contention was a proposed 6,000-square-foot video board—later reduced to 4,600 square feet—that would inconvenience those whom the Cubs annoyingly call "our rooftop partners"—the people who sell seats atop buildings across from the ballpark.

For many years before 2004, these people had been pocketing all the profits from stealing the Cubs' product—the entertainment value of Major League Baseball—and selling this product to fans, many of whom could purchase admission to Wrigley Field but preferred the rooftop festivities. In 2004, the Cubs and the "rooftop partners" struck a twenty-year deal under which the Cubs receive 17 percent of what their partners make. It is unclear by what peculiar theory of property rights these "partners" acquired a claim on a portion of the value of what the Cubs produce.

John Locke, who had a lot more to do with the invention of this republic than Abner Doubleday had to do with the invention of baseball, said that one acquires property in, for example, land by mixing one's labor with it, thereby improving it. Lockean theory links the acquisition of any property to one's own labor. How, one wonders, do the "rooftop partners" gain their property interest in Cubs baseball? By what labor do the "rooftop partners" gain this property interest, other than the "labor" of owning the buildings and constructing bleacher seats from which their customers can watch the team that the "rooftop partners" did nothing to build? This may be of merely academic interest, but by 2013 it was interfering with the Cubs' attempts to compete with teams that were nourished by newer, more money-generating ballparks.

The rooftops are sports bars with nice views, and Tom Ricketts has invested in one just to see what the business is about. It is about grossing $25 million a year, which is what the rooftop partners report. It is conceivable that the real figure is north of $30 million. One rooftop that was bought for $36,000 in 1980 is comparable to another that in 2011 sold for $4.8 million. In May 2012, a USA Today reporter watched a game from a Sheffield Avenue rooftop. But the one he watched was a Chicago Bulls NBA play-off game. There were many empty seats in Wrigley as the Cubs played the Texas Rangers—it was a makeup game for one postponed because of bad weather—but on the rooftop, "the bar was packed" with Bulls fans high-fiving one another as the Bulls upset the Miami Heat. The reporter noted, "These patrons might have paid $70–$150 for their rooftop view, but they still preferred watching the Bulls on plasma TVs [to] the Cubs in person."

In 1988, when the Cubs finally turned on the lights, sensible Cub fans said: It's about time. The resistance to night games came not just, and understandably, from residents of the neighborhood but also from fans who seemed attached less to the Cubs than to the idea of the Cubs as a kind of baseball Williamsburg—a quaint evocation of a bygone era. In 2013, when the question was whether the Cubs would be allowed to install the video board in left field and other signage, Tom Ricketts said the ball club could succeed if, and only if, it could treat Wrigley Field as a revenue-generating institution rather than as a "museum." He said the new signs would produce $20 million a year, a sum that could purchase some helpful on-field talent. And only talent would reverse a troubling trend: In the previous three seasons, 2010 through 2012, Cubs attendance had declined by about 3,000 tickets a game, to 35,600. Multiply 3,000 by the price of a ticket plus a hot dog and an Old Style, and multiply that by 81. Serious money is at issue.

As commonly used when speaking of sports, the word "professional" simply means "not amateur." Professional sports are, the *Oxford English Dictionary* says, "engaged in for money." But another common usage of "professional" means "expert," implying adherence to exacting standards. There has been professional baseball, in the first sense, for more than a century and a half. But Major League Baseball has become markedly more professional, in the second sense, in recent decades. It is not a coincidence that this has occurred as the sums of money at stake have grown much larger. Baseball has always generated, pitch by pitch and game by game, season after season, a vast sea of data. Only recently has this been gathered and used systematically. And new ballparks have been built to accommodate baseball's increased professionalism.

These ballparks have weight-training and exercise machines, supervised by strength coaches, innovations that would have horrified many generations of baseball people, if the possibilities had even occurred to them. Until relatively recently—well after the Second World War— baseball's conventional wisdom held that the way to get into condition to play baseball was to play baseball. A corollary dogma advised players to avoid weight training, lest they become "muscle-bound" and lose flexibility.

New ballparks have multiple batting cages in tunnels beneath the stands and close enough to the dugout so that players can hone their swings between at bats and pinch hitters can limber up. New ballparks have video facilities, often close to the dugout, where even during the game players can see video of their recent at bats, or of the opposing pitcher's offerings, or of the way that day's home plate umpire is defining the strike zone. Wrigley Field at one hundred has none of these things. The only batting cage is under the outfield bleachers and must be reached by walking across the playing field, so it cannot be used during a game. It is simply more difficult for Cubs players than for any of their National League rivals to—in the players' patois—"get their work in." This means that because of Wrigley Field's cozy configuration, the team is at a competitive disadvantage. This defect will have been rectified by the time Wrigley is 102 years old.

Wrigleyville has an agreeable middle-class feel to it, but the median price of a home in the neighborhood is almost $1 million. It is difficult to image that a 175-room boutique hotel adjacent to the ballpark, plus a spruced-up Sheffield Avenue used as a pedestrian mall on game days, will damage property values. But beyond being respectful of the neighborhood, and assuaging its anxieties, the challenge for Ricketts is to preserve the Wrigley Field of 1914 while making it suitable for the fans—and the players, managers, and coaches—of 2014.

When Wrigley was built, ballparks were simple edifices for providing paying customers with vantage points—mostly bench seats, sometimes folding chairs—from which to watch a game. Each ballpark had only one significant revenue stream: ticket sales. Players expected from the ballpark only a satisfactory playing surface and, maybe—in some cities, visiting players put on their uniforms at their hotels—places to dress before the game and to shower after it. Today, however, baseball—the game itself—has become much more demanding of the players, who in turn demand more of their workplace. Fans demand comforts beyond peanuts and Cracker Jack, including entertainment between innings and even Internet access. The ballpark itself is a complex machine for generating better player performances, more satisfying fan experiences, and rivers of revenue to buy better players who will keep the fans coming through the turnstiles and tuning in to the teams' broadcasts.

A proper twenty-first-century ballpark offers Wi-Fi because most of the fans settle into their seats with smartphones in their pockets, and more and more fans also have electronic tablets in hand to serve their insatiable appetites for information. Suppose the guy sitting next to you cannot remember the name of the Cub player who was traded for himself? Piece of cake. Noodle around with Google and you will come to Dickie Noles, who on September 22, 1987, was traded by the Cubs to the Tigers for a player to be named later. On September 26, in the ninth inning, the Tigers brought him in to pitch to the Blue Jays' Juan Beniquez with the bases loaded. Beniquez hit a walk-off triple. The Tigers soon designated Noles to be the player named later and shipped him back to the Cubs.

If the woman to your left wonders what game might have been the greatest ever played at Wrigley Field, Google "May 2, 1917, Wrigley Field." For nine innings on that day in the Cubs' second year in Wrigley Field, Cubs pitcher James "Hippo" Vaughn and Reds pitcher Fred Toney, a former Cub, tossed no-hitters, something that had never happened before and has not happened since. In the tenth inning, the Reds' leadoff batter got a hit, and then some bad Cubs defensive plays (one of them on a ball hit by Cincinnati's Jim Thorpe, the decathlon champion at the 1912 Olympics in Stockholm) led to a Reds run. The Cubs did not score in the bottom of the tenth. The game lasted just one hour and fifty minutes.

Why do so many of us care so much about professional sports teams and, hence, about the buildings in which they practice their craft for pay? One answer is: We are more tribal than we, in our modern vanity, like to acknowledge. Which means Senator Daniel Patrick Moynihan was right about what he called "the liberal expectancy."

The most accomplished intellectual in politics since John Quincy Adams, and a New York and New Deal liberal in good standing, Moynihan was fascinated by the durable role of ethnicity in our nation of immigrants, and in the larger world. Beginning in the nineteenth century, he said, the "liberal expectancy" gripped much of the intelligentsia. The expectancy was that as science advanced in tandem with the rationality of societies in which markets allocate wealth and opportunity, the forces that propelled history in preindustrial ages—principally, religion and ethnicity—would lose their saliency. This has not happened, which suggests that human nature is not as changeable as many people hoped and others expected or feared. Perhaps we are creatures built—hardwired, in the current argot—for primal allegiances. And perhaps there is much about the modern world that does not satisfy this ancient but still potent yearning for group memberships and collective affinities.

Moynihan was one of my closest friends, and I can attest that he was almost immune to the translation of his vestigial tribalism—if he had any—into sports allegiances. He and his wife, Liz, owned a modest rural home in Delaware County, in upstate New York, not far from Cooperstown. I once toured the Hall of Fame with him and can report that although the shrine and its worshippers piqued his sociological imagination, he was otherwise unstirred.

The only time I saw his passions engaged by anything about sports was when a New Jersey senator had the audacity to propose having June 19 declared National Baseball Day. This senator alleged that on this day in 1846, "baseball's first game was played," supposedly at Elysian Fields in Hoboken, New Jersey, between two organized teams from across the Hudson River in Manhattan. The senator did not explain how, or why, two teams had been organized—one of them began playing in Madison Square in 1842—prior to baseball's "first game."

Moynihan, committed to senatorial courtesy and oblivious to his own state's stake in this, at first supported the New Jersey senator's measure. Fortunately, some people more attuned than Moynihan to things sporting alerted him to the peril to which he was exposing himself. He promptly rose in defense of Cooperstown's spurious claim to be baseball's birthplace. His argument, which he considered crushing, was: "Baseball was born in Cooperstown in 1839. The New York State highway sign near Doubleday Field outside the Hall of Fame says so." QED.

The prosaic truth, however, is that young Abner, then twenty, spent the summer of 1839 155 miles southeast of Cooperstown, at West Point, where he was a plebe. The only thing he started, with some hostile help, was the Civil War, as everyone knows who has read the historical marker at Fort Sumter. It says that on April 12, 1861, he was an artillery captain. The national pastime, like the nation itself, was fertilized by the bloodshed of the Civil War. "Baseball," wrote A. Bartlett Giamatti, "grew during the surge to fraternalism—to fraternal societies, sodalities, associations, and aggregations—that followed the fratricide." The sport "showed who had won the war and where the country was building, which was in the industrial cities of the North." Then baseball flourished through rivalries between teams organized around factories or ethnic social organizations. When General Doubleday—as he had become in long service that took him to, among other places, Gettysburg— died, in 1893, full of years and honors, a long obituary in the *New York Times* made no mention of baseball, there being no known connection, then or now, between it and him.

Nevertheless, Moynihan was politically prudent in defending the creation myth that is commercially lucrative for some upstate constituents. And perhaps Moynihan was also moved by New York chauvinism. In which case he was, after all, somewhat tribal, and therefore was evidence for his theory about the fallacy of the liberal expectancy. Be that as it may, Wrigley Field is powerful, if redundant, evidence against this expectancy. As are all the other ballparks where people cluster for the pleasure of suspending their rationality and indulging their tribalism for a few hours.

Bart Giamatti was a Falstaffian figure with a robust appetite for baseball, martinis, and other admirable pleasures. He became baseball's seventh commissioner in September 1988. He died of a heart attack on September 1, 1989, after the arduous negotiation that led to the lifetime ban of Pete Rose as punishment for betting on baseball. For nine years Giamatti was president of Yale University, where he was a scholar of the Renaissance. His last book, published shortly before his death, was *Take Time for Paradise: Americans and Their Games*. Its themes explain why we care, and why it is reasonable to care, about a place like Wrigley Field.

Giamatti believed that we make too little of sport when we make too much of it. That is, when we try to infuse sport with too much meaning. When we encrust it with theory and weigh it down with transcendent functions, we obscure its real purpose "as a shared moment of leisure." Which, properly understood, is rather a lot and quite enough.

The wisdom here is this: The beauty of sport is its *absence* of meaning. With sport, an individual, a team, or a community experiences the kind of happiness that arises, Giamatti said, from a rare and fleeting "absence of care." This can be sensed so intensely that it invites comparison to religious experiences. This tempts some people, he noted, to postulate that "the sports experience must be the tattered remnants" of what earlier, less disenchanted ages considered religious experiences. Giamatti believed that sport is "ultimately subversive of religion." This is so because, whereas religion concerns the most consequential things, "sport cares not for religion's *consequences*. Sport cares only for itself."

Rather than encumber sport with religious echoes, it is better, Giamatti said, to understand sport as one of those "shared activities that have no purpose except fully to be themselves." Sports achievements, however luminous, are never perfect. They are, however, "uncommon enough to remain a bright spot in the memory, thus creating a reservoir of transformation to which we can return when we are free to do so." This transformation is one purpose of recreation, which means re-creation.

In Shakespeare's *Henry IV*, Prince Hal tells us—warns us, really—that "if all the year were playing holidays, to sport would be as tedious as to work." For all but a fortunate few, who live to work rather than work to live, work is tedious. It is so—the French word for work is *travail*—because it is a necessity rather than a choice. The reason leisure is, Giamatti thought, an index of a culture's condition is that leisure is about making free choices. Work is necessary; leisure is an escape from necessitousness. There are those who say that since the coming of the Industrial Revolution, sport has become industrial. And they say sport has become, in Giamatti's phrase, "junk food for the spirit," a narcotic, another opiate of the masses. Giamatti, however, summoned Aristotle for the defense: "We do without leisure . . . only to give ourselves leisure." That is, we work so that we may play. There is, said Giamatti, a progression "from what is necessary to what is desirable." The people who make the effort to come together as a crowd at a sporting event do so because they desire to become a community, "a small town of people sharing neither work nor pain nor deprivation nor anger but the common experience of being released to enjoy the moment." There is enjoyment even in disappointment and defeat because the sports fan is part of a group of the similarly affected. At a sporting event, when we, a voluntary gathering of strangers, are pulled to our feet by admiration, we *feel* together what we *see* together. And what we feel "begins as a gnawing hunger and becomes a rage to perfection." If, Giamatti said, "perfection" is too strong, then: "a rage to get it right." So, in a sense, we go to the ballpark to become better.

Today sports are "city-bound" in that they are connected to cities. It may seem odd that Giamatti linked the sport he adored with cities, because he called baseball "the most strenuously nostalgic of all our sports, the most traditionally conscious of tradition, the most intent on enshrining its rural origins." But one "rural" setting of baseball's origins, where the Knickerbockers played, is now near the

Murray Hill neighborhood of Manhattan. About cities, Giamatti was unsentimental:

> A city is not an extended family. That is a tribe or a clan. A city is a collection of disparate families who agree to a fiction: they agree to live *as if* they were as close in blood or ties of kinship as in fact they are in physical proximity. . . . It is a considerable pact, a city. If a family is an expression of continuity through biology, a city is an expression of continuity through will and imagination. . . . Sports and cities share a common characteristic: They are deeply conventional.

Sports are rules-bound activities, "precision in counterpoint with passion," and "stability vying with volatility." Baseball's conventions, Giamatti believed, mirror "the condition of freedom" for Americans. We are "free enough to consent to an order that will enhance and compound—as it constrains—our freedom." So in every game, as "energy and order merge," baseball "fulfills the promise America made to itself to cherish the individual while recognizing the overarching claims of the group" as "we re-create our daily portion of freedom, in public."

It is, of course, a transitory creation. Even the competitors are almost evanescent, because for athletes sport compresses life's normal trajectory of aspiration, attainment, and decline. But when the contest has ended, the

memory lingers on. And the memory of something difficult done well is enough. The contest should be spared
the burden of carrying too much meaning, or the wrong
kinds of meanings. For a century, Wrigley Field has been
a memory-making place for afternoon and evening communities. Hence the complex sentiments and associations
that this simple North Side structure stirs.

Which is why we care so much about what happens in
places like Wrigley Field. What happens, really? It *is* just a
game. Yes, like any craft, it is worth doing well. And excellence, wherever it occurs, is worth savoring and honoring.
But, in spite of the unending attempts of metaphysicians
in the bleachers and press boxes to make sport more than
it is, the real appeal of it for spectators is that sport enables
us, for a few hours, to step out of the river of time and into
a pastime.

Which is not to say that sports—particularly professional sports, and especially baseball, with its enchanting
everydayness—serve no valuable function. Utility, however,
is not the same thing as meaning. Professional sports teams
are municipal assets. They are public utilities that can help
infuse a dust of individuals with a unifying sense of tame
tribalism. Or, as in the case of Chicago, sports allegiances

can transform a fragile mosaic of mutually wary neighbor-hoods into something like a community, one united, albeit tenuously and intermittently, by a shared vocabulary of af-fections, loyalties, hopes, and anxieties.

This is why there are many people—many millions, in fact—who rarely or never visit Wrigley Field but for whom this venue is nevertheless somehow important. Similarly, the United States Capitol and the Statue of Liberty are, for scores of millions of Americans who never visit them, re-minders of what it means to be an American. For the subset of Americans who are baseball fans, Wrigley Field is an ori-enting patrimony. For this cohort, it is pleasant just know-ing that the ballpark has been there for a very long time, that it will be there for a long time, and that they could one day choose to drop by and enjoy it.

When my son Geoff and his wife, Maia, who then lived in the Chicago suburb of Naperville, had their first child, I argued strenuously for them to give the boy a boost into life by giving him the resonant name Clark Addison Will. They rejected this terrific idea, not because they consid-ered it weird but because they knew it was banal. Appar-ently, lots of parents have given children those melodious names. In September 2007, Paul and Teri Fields of Michi-gan City, Indiana, named their bouncing baby boy Wrig-ley. And in December 2008, when Brian and Lauren Clark of Plainfield, Illinois, had their first child, a daughter, they named her Addison Nicole. When she uses her middle initial, she will be Addison N. Clark. The five children of

Ralph and Julie Dynek of Northfield, Illinois, are named Addison, Clark, Sheffield, Grace Waveland, and Ivy. It is a rare place that inspires such tributes of affection.

More than twenty major league ballparks that opened *after* Wrigley Field did have been demolished. In fact, more than ten parks that opened as recently as the 1960s and 1970s are gone. Wrigley endures, and about 140 million people have watched games there, a lot more than the approximately 99 million persons who lived in America in 1914. Wrigley has lasted because it is, like a clipper ship, elegantly practical. If architecture is, as Goethe said, frozen music, then Wrigley Field is a rendering, in bricks and structural steel, of "Take Me Out to the Ball Game."

With that sentiment I have come perilously close to the cardinal sin of gushing, so I shall subside. But not before urging you to take the El to the Addison stop and see for yourself what all the fuss is about.

I began this rumination on Wrigley Field with the words of a poet. I will conclude with words from another one: "Life is a long preparation for something that never happens." Forlorn Cub fans waiting for a World Series may agree with William Butler Yeats, but what he wrote is not quite right. Life *is* what happens, whatever it is. Anticipation of what might happen next is part of the fun. And life, which has its ups and downs, is leavened by the pleasure of passing time now and then in nice places, like the little one on the North Side.

Notes

7 **"Architecture is inhabited sculpture"**: Robert I. Fitzhenry, *The Harper Book of Quotations*, 3rd ed. (New York: Harper-Collins, 1993), 42.

11 **"I would have written of me on my stone"**: Ibid., 123.

12 **The *Chicago Tribune* that morning reported**: Edward Burns, "Cubs Waste Two Home Runs in 4 to 3 Setback," *Chicago Tribune*, May 4, 1941, B1.

13 **The ad told the unvarnished truth**: Display ad, *Chicago Tribune*, August 30, 1948, B3.

14 **"Architecture, of all the arts"**: Ernest Dimnet, *What We Live By* (New York: Simon & Schuster, 1932), 141.
Clark, along the third-base side: Don Hayner and Tom McNamee, *Streetwise Chicago: A History of Chicago Street Names* (Chicago: Loyola University Press, 1988), 1, 23, 117, 131.

18 **Champaign and Urbana are cheek by jowl**: Dannel McCollum, "Champaign: The Creation of a City of Champaign," City of Champaign, http://ci.champaign.il.us/about-champaign/history/creation-of-champaign/.

21 **If Chicago, a no-nonsense city of prose**: I draw on several collections of Carl Sandburg's works, including *Chicago*

Poems (1916) and *Smoke and Steel* (1920), available here: http://www.bartleby.com/people/Sandburg.html.

22 **Of Sandburg's thick and weird "biography":** Sean Wilentz, *The Best American History Essays on Lincoln* (New York: Palgrave Macmillan, 2009), 51.

26 **The journal he kept throughout his life:** David Lilienthal, *The Journals of David E. Lilienthal: The TVA Years, 1939–1945* (New York: Evanston, 1964), 2.

The late Julian Simon, an economist: Julian Simon, *The Ultimate Resource 2* (Princeton: Princeton University Press, 1996), 236.

27 **Lou "the Mad Russian" Novikoff, who played:** Richard Cahan and Mark Jacob, *The Game That Was: The George Brace Baseball Photo Collection* (Chicago: Contemporary Books, 1996), 234.

30 **When Eddie Sawyer, who managed the Phillies:** W. C. Heinz, "Stan Musial's Last Day," *Life*, October 11, 1963, 98.

31 **"Boston is mourning":** Peter Levine, A. G. *Spalding and the Rise of Baseball* (New York: Oxford University Press, 1985), 21.

32 **A Chicago chauvinist:** John Thorn, *Baseball in the Garden of Eden: The Secret History of the Early Game* (New York: Simon & Schuster, 2011), 155.

As Peter Levine writes: Levine, A. G. *Spalding*, 23.

33 **"One of his less successful ideas":** Peter Golenbock, *Wrigleyville: A Magical History Tour of the Chicago Cubs* (New York: St. Martin's Press, 1996), 23.

34 **An 1889 editorial in the *Spalding Guide*:** Ibid., 62.
Golenbock notes that Chicago's shopping center: Ibid.
But long before any ballpark had lights: Ibid., 62–63.
This was pursuant to Spalding's insistence: Ibid., 91–92.

36 **According to Golenbock, at about this time:** Ibid., 99.

37 **According to one of baseball's durable myths:** Art Ahrens,

Chicago Cubs: Tinker to Evers to Chance (Charleston: Arcadia, 2007), 73–74.

42 **In F. Scott Fitzgerald's *The Great Gatsby*:** F. Scott Fitzgerald, *The Great Gatsby* (New York: Scribner, 1925), 71–73.

43 **In his 1962 memoir, *Veeck as in Wreck*:** Bill Veeck, *Veeck as in Wreck: The Autobiography of Bill Veeck*, with Ed Linn (Chicago: University of Chicago Press, 1962), 35–36.

44 **When Judge Kenesaw Mountain Landis:** Roberts Ehrgott, *Mr. Wrigley's Ball Club: Chicago and the Cubs During the Jazz Age* (Lincoln: University of Nebraska Press, 2013), 263. **The student who invited him:** Ibid., 78.

45 **Wrigley's father made soap:** Golenbock, *Wrigleyville*, 173–74.

46 **Wrigley was excessively fond of saying:** Ibid., 200.
To be sure, the Supreme Court: See: *Federal Baseball Club v. National League*, 259 U.S. 200 (1922).
But as the late Jim Murray: Thom Loverro, *Home of the Game: The Story of Camden Yards* (Dallas: Taylor, 1999), xii.

47 **Radio stations were multiplying rapidly:** Herman S. Hettinger, *A Decade of Radio Advertising* (Chicago: University of Chicago Press, 1933).
"By mid-1929": Ehrgott, *Mr. Wrigley's Ball Club*, 95.

48 **One farmer within range of a Chicago station:** Ibid, 50.

49 **This was dramatized on the city's lakefront:** See, for example: "Figures and Facts on the Fight Tonight," *Chicago Tribune*, September 22, 1927, 1, and "Famous Fans at Famous Battle Air Their Views," *Chicago Tribune*, September 23, 1927, 12.

50 **Ehrgott reports that during the 1920s:** Ehrgott, *Mr. Wrigley's Ball Club*, 3.

51 **The idea was Ladies' Day:** Ibid., 53.

52 **"I spend $1.5 million a year":** Ibid., 55.

But the Cubs still ran ads in the *Tribune*: Ibid., 48–49.

53 **Wrigley, who said, "It is easier to control":** Golenbock, *Wrigleyville*, 214.

54 **Which is why a Chicago newspaper:** Ibid., 215.

In July 1926, the *Chicago Tribune*: Ehrgott, *Mr. Wrigley's Ball Club*, 288.

When Abraham Lincoln met Harriet Beecher Stowe: See, for example: Susan Belasco, "Harriet Beecher Stowe," *New York Times*, http://topics.nytimes.com/top/reference/timestopics/people/s/harriet_beecher_stowe/index.html.

56 **A good tutor about this episode is Leigh Montville:** Leigh Montville, *The Big Bam: The Life and Times of Babe Ruth* (Broadway Books, 2007). For Montville's full explanation, see pages 309–12.

57 **Having written a farewell note:** Ibid., 309.

The judge presiding over a dispute: Ehrgott, *Mr. Wrigley's Ball Club*, 346.

58 **The Cubs, Montville writes:** Montville, *The Big Bam*, 309.

59 **But the Scripps Howard News Service:** Paul Dickson, *The Dickson Baseball Dictionary*, 3rd. ed. (New York: Norton, 2009), 157–58.

In his 1955 autobiography, *The Tumult and the Shouting*: See Montville, *The Big Bam*, 312–13, for Grantland Rice's autobiographical account of Ruth's story.

65 **The headline on the obituary:** Bruce Weber, "Ruth Ann Steinhagen Is Dead at 83; Shot a Ballplayer," *New York Times*, March 24, 2013, A22.

68 **He was a human fireplug:** Arthur Daley, "Sports of the Times: A Tragic Figure," *New York Times*, November 25, 1948, 52.

70 **An often-told story:** See, for example, Richard O'Mara, "Like a Bat Out of Hell," *Baltimore Sun*, September 4, 1998, http://articles.baltimoresun.com/1998-09-04/features/1998247062_1_hack-wilson-baseball-robert/2, and Bob Her-

zog, "Wilson's Record May Be the Most Awesome of All Time," *Los Angeles Times*, August 2, 1998, http://articles .latimes.com/1998/aug/02/sports/sp-9571.

Wilson said, "I never played drunk": Glenn Stout, *The Cubs: The Complete Story of Chicago Cubs Baseball* (New York: Houghton Mifflin, 2007), 128.

But Bill Veeck remembered one instance: Veeck, *Veeck as in Wreck*, 32.

71 **After the game, when a boy:** "1929 World Series," Baseball-Reference.com, http://www.baseball-reference.com/bullpen/ 1929_World_Series.

74 **"In modern baseball":** Bill James, *The New Bill James Historical Baseball Abstract* (New York: Free Press, 2001), 736.

75 **Recalling the winter of 1930:** Ira Berkow, "On Baseball; Hack Wilson's Lesson Still Valid," *New York Times*, September 5, 1998, D3.

76 **Shortly before his death, Wilson:** Clifton Blue Parker, *Fouled Away: The Baseball Tragedy of Hack Wilson* (Jefferson, NC: McFarland, 2000), 2.

78 **When, in 1934, he became:** Andrew Steele, "Philip Wrigley," Society for American Baseball Research, http://sabr .org/bioproj/person/1043052b.

79 **Carefully parse the words Philip said:** Ibid.

In 1958, Wrigley told *Sports Illustrated*: Robert Boyle, "A Shy Man at a Picnic," *Sports Illustrated*, April 14, 1958.

80 **Charlie Grimm, who played for the Cubs:** Golenbock, *Wrigleyville*, 271.

"It was," Wrigley said: Boyle, "A Shy Man."

Loyalty to a Chicago friend: Ibid.

82 **This venture inspired the 1992 movie:** *A League of Their Own*; quotations taken from Internet Movie Database, http://www.imdb.com/title/tt0104694/quotes.

An ad Wrigley placed in Chicago newspapers: Display ad, *Chicago Tribune*, August 30, 1948, B3.

Winning was not central: Steele, "Philip Wrigley."

"His slogan was 'Come Out and Have a Picnic'": Golenbock, *Wrigleyville*, 357.

83 He told *Sports Illustrated*: Boyle, "A Shy Man."

In 1958, Wrigley explained: Ibid.

84 "*A doctor can bury his mistakes*": Fitzhenry, *Harper Book of Quotations*, 43.

Its origin story is told by Bill Veeck Jr. : For quotations throughout this section, I drew on Veeck, *Veeck as in Wreck*.

89 That team frequently played in front of such small crowds: Kathy O'Malley and Dorothy Collin, "Daleyville," *Chicago Tribune*, April 3, 1991.

On September 17, 1937: Edward Burns, "New Wrigley Field Blooms in Scenic Beauty—and Scoffers Rush to Apologize," *Chicago Tribune*, September 12, 1937, B5.

Paul Dickson is the author: Paul Dickson, *Bill Veeck: Baseball's Greatest Maverick* (New York: Walker, 2012).

90 Veeck said the Cubs assigned: Ibid., 42–43.

91 Paul Sullivan, who has been covering baseball: For several quotations and anecdotes throughout this section, I drew on correspondence with Paul Sullivan.

93 Santa Catalina, the "isle with the smile": Ehrgott, *Mr. Wrigley's Ball Club*, 154.

94 He had dinner in Los Angeles: Ronald Reagan, *An American Life: An Autobiography* (New York: Simon & Schuster, 1990).

96 In his 1990 memoir: Ibid.

98 In 1907, when the Cubs ruled the roost: Edward A. Berlin, *King of Ragtime: Scott Joplin and His Era* (New York: Oxford University Press, 1994), 76.

99 In the summer of 1919: William M. Tuttle Jr., "Contested Neighborhoods and Racial Violence: Prelude to the Chicago Riot of 1919," *Journal of Negro History*, vol. 55, no. 4 (October 1970), 282.

101 **On Monday, May 19, 1947:** Edward Burns, "Record 46,572 See Dodgers Beat Cubs, 4–2," *Chicago Tribune*, May 19, 1947, 29.

102 **The headline in the *Chicago Defender*:** Ron Grossman, "'42' in the Windy City," *Chicago Tribune*, April 28, 2013.

103 **A Cub official told the paper:** Leslie A. Heaphy, *Black Baseball and Chicago: Essays on the Players, Teams and Games* (Jefferson, NC: McFarland, 2006), 184.

That day, Mike Royko: Mike Royko, *One More Time: The Best of Mike Royko* (Chicago: University of Chicago Press, 1999), 68–70.

106 **"Managers," Wrigley said, "are expendable":** Steele, "Philip Wrigley."

Wrigley's rationale was: Stout, *The Cubs*, 236.

108 **For the 1966 season, he hired Leo Durocher:** Al Yellon, Kasey Ignarski, and Matthew Silverman, *Cubs by the Numbers: A Complete Team History of the Chicago Cubs by Uniform* (New York: Skyhorse, 2009).

109 **His salty memoir:** For quotations throughout this section, I drew on Leo Durocher, *Nice Guys Finish Last*, with Ed Linn (Chicago: University of Chicago Press, 2009).

115 **The Cardinals sent out another scout:** George Vecsey, *Stan Musial: An American Life* (New York: ESPN Books / Ballantine Books, 2011), 202.

"Can't act. Slightly bald": Mike Towle, *Pete Rose: Baseball's Charlie Hustle* (Nashville: Cumberland House, 2003), 37.

116 **Banks said that when Saperstein:** Golenbock, *Wrigleyville*, 349.

118 **"His wrists," said a teammate:** "Ernie Banks," Baseball Library.com, http://www.baseballlibrary.com/ballplayers/player.php?name=ernie_banks_1931.

119 **Bill James, in the first version:** James, *Historical Baseball Abstract*, 367.

120 **In 1958, an opposing manager:** Golenbock, *Wrigleyville*, 349.

121 **According to Golenbock, Caray was fired:** Ibid., 456.

122 **Nearly forty years after he first experienced it:** For several quotations and anecdotes throughout this section, I drew on correspondence with Mike Krukow.

124 **As his wife settled into her seat:** For several quotations and anecdotes throughout this section, I drew on Tyler Kepner, "On a Sunny Day at Wrigley, a Perfect Storm of Offense," *New York Times*, May 17, 2009, SP1.

In Ashburn's final big league season: David H. Nathan, *The McFarland Baseball Quotations Dictionary* (Jefferson, NC: McFarland, 2000), 13.

125 **It is somehow fitting:** For this and other Danny Ozark quotations, see Robert Cohen, *The 50 Greatest Players in New York Yankees History* (Plymouth, UK: Scarecrow, 2012), 32, and Dickson, *Dickson Baseball Dictionary*, 619.

126 **April is—a poet born and raised in the Midwest said:** See T. S. Eliot's *The Waste Land* (1922), available here: http://www.bartleby.com/201/1.html.

Because it is the most famous rhetorical moment: "Lee Elia Cubs Rant," Nuttysportsvideos, available here: http://www.youtube.com/watch?v=8S0CDtEz_Bo.

129 **What is not well known:** For several quotations and anecdotes throughout this section, I drew on correspondence with Keith Moreland.

130 **In 1984, one of the happier summers:** For quotations and attendance numbers throughout this section, I drew on Tobias J. Moskowitz and L. Jon Wertheim, *Scorecasting: The Hidden Influences Behind How Sports Are Played and Games Are Won* (New York: Three Rivers, 2011).

138 **Then, according to the Discovery Channel:** For much of the information related to beer in this section, I drew on

Martyn Ives, *How Beer Saved the World* (Discovery Channel, 2011); Steven Johnson, *The Ghost Map: The Story of London's Most Terrifying Epidemic—and How It Changed Science, Cities, and the Modern World* (New York: Riverhead, 2006); George F. Will, "Hooding Remarks" (Princeton University, June 4, 2012), http://www.princeton.edu/main/news/archive/S33/88/44Q33/; and Daniel Okrent, *Last Call: The Rise and Fall of Prohibition* (New York: Scribner, 2010).

148 **Before the game, he waxed poetic:** For Vin Scully's opening remarks, see Curt Smith, *Pull Up a Chair: The Vin Scully Story* (Dulles, VA: Potomac Books, 2009); Steve Nidetz, "Despite Blowout in Game 1, Big Audience Got a Fine Show," *Chicago Tribune*, October 6, 1989; and "This Time It Will Be Better," *Desipio Blog*, October 1, 2007, http://www.desipio.com/?p=1390.

149 **This is Miss Havisham as seen:** Charles Dickens, *Great Expectations* (Hertfordshire, UK: Wordsworth Editions Limited, 2000), 48–49.

150 **The Cubs were leading the 2003:** For much of the information related to the Bartman incident in this section, I drew on Alex Gibney, *Catching Hell* (ESPN Films, 2011).

151 **The relevant rule reads:** "2013 Official Baseball Rules: 2.00 Definition of Terms," Major League Baseball, 2013, http://mlb.mlb.com/mlb/downloads/y2013/official_base ball_rules.pdf, 18.

155 **In *Chicago: City on the Make*:** Nelson Algren, *Chicago: City on the Make* (New York: Doubleday, 1951), 30.

156 **In a *New Yorker* cartoon:** George F. Will, "Your Brain on Cubs," *Newsweek*, March 29, 2008.

157 **So says Jordan Grafman:** Dan Gordon, ed., *Your Brain on Cubs: Inside the Heads of Players and Fans* (New York: Dana, 2008).

164 **On October 23, 1943:** Winston S. Churchill, *Never Give In! The Best of Winston Churchill's Speeches* (New York: Hyperion, 2003), 358–61.

165 **It was, after all, a great Chicago architect:** Fitzhenry, *Harper Book of Quotations*, 43.

166 **Returning to the huddle:** Mark C. Bodanza, *1933: Football at the Depth of the Great Depression* (Bloomington: iUniverse, 2010), 27.

167 **To those who said, "You can't turn back":** For information related to Janet Marie Smith, I drew on several sources, including correspondence with Janet Marie Smith; Ryan Vaillancourt, "Janet Marie Smith and the Changes to Dodger Stadium," *Los Angeles Downtown News*, February 12, 2013, http://www.ladowntownnews.com/news/janet-marie-smith-and-the-changes-to-dodger-stadium/article_41c5419e-7245-11e2-9350-0019bb2963f4.html; Bret McCabe, "Janet Marie Smith Talks Ballparks and Urban Transformation," *Hub*, December 7, 2012, http://hub.jhu.edu/2012/12/07/berman-lecture-smith-ballparks; and Ryan Sharrow, "Power 20: Janet Marie Smith," *Balitmore Business Journal*, February 18, 2011, http://www.bizjournals.com/baltimore/print-edition/2011/02/18/power-20-janet-marie-smith.html?page=all.

170 **He says "the best $50,000 we spent":** Martan F. Nolan, "Advice to Red Sox: Just Keep Swinging," *Boston Globe*, September 1, 2001.

172 **His grandfather was the wit:** George F. Will, *Bunts: Curt Flood, Camden Yards, Pete Rose and Other Reflections on Baseball* (New York: Touchstone, 1999), 91.

173 **William Zinsser, a gifted writer:** William Zinsser, *The Writer Who Stayed* (Philadelphia: Paul Dry Books, 2012), 66, 124–25.

174 **In it he recalls the pleasure:** Ralph Branca, *A Moment*

in Time: An American Story of Baseball, Heartbreak, and Grace, with David Ritz (New York: Scribner, 2011), 25.

177 **He said owning the team:** For various facts related to Wrigley Field and Tom Ricketts in this section, I drew on correspondence with Tom Ricketts.

180 **In May 2012, a USA *Today*:** Bob Nightengale, "No Joy in Wrigleyville as Cubs, Neighbors Clash," *USA Today*, May 9, 2013.

187 **"Baseball," wrote A. Bartlett Giamatti:** A. Bartlett Giamatti, *A Great and Glorious Game: Baseball Writings of A. Bartlett Giamatti* (Chapel Hill: Algonquin, 1998), 46.

188 **Its themes explain why we care:** For quotations throughout this section, I drew on A. Bartlett Giamatti, *Take Time for Paradise: Americans and Their Games* (New York: Bloomsbury USA, 1989).

194 **"Life is a long preparation":** Fitzhenry, *Harper Book of Quotations*, 263.

Throughout this book, records, standings, payroll figures, information about ballparks, and other miscellaneous data have been drawn from:

Correspondence with Steve Hirdt, Elias Sports Bureau

Correspondence with Michael Haupert, University of Wisconsin, La Crosse

http://www.baseball-almanac.com/

http://www.baseball-reference.com/

http://www.ballparksofbaseball.com/

http://mlb.mlb.com/home

http://www.retrosheet.org/

http://sabr.org/research/

Bibliography

Ahrens, Art. *Chicago Cubs: Tinker to Evers to Chance*. Charleston: Arcadia, 2007.

Algren, Nelson. *Chicago: City on the Make*. New York: Doubleday, 1951.

Ballparks of Baseball: http://www.ballparksofbaseball.com/.

Baseball Almanac: http://www.baseball-almanac.com/.

Baseball-Reference.com: http://www.baseball-reference.com/.

Belasco, Susan. "Harriet Beecher Stowe." *New York Times*. http://topics.nytimes.com/top/reference/timestopics/people/s/harriet_beecher_stowe/index.html.

Berkow, Ira. "On Baseball; Hack Wilson's Lesson Still Valid." *New York Times*, September 5, 1998, D3.

Berlin, Edward A. *King of Ragtime: Scott Joplin and His Era*. New York: Oxford University Press, 1994.

Bodanza, Mark C. *1933: Football at the Depth of the Great Depression*. Bloomington: iUniverse, 2010.

Boyle, Robert. "A Shy Man at a Picnic." *Sports Illustrated*, April 14, 1958.

Branca, Ralph. *A Moment in Time: An American Story of Baseball, Heartbreak, and Grace*. With David Ritz. New York: Scribner, 2011.

Burns, Edward. "Cubs Waste Two Home Runs in 4 to 3 Setback." *Chicago Tribune*, May 4, 1941, B1.

———. "New Wrigley Field Blooms in Scenic Beauty—and Scoffers Rush to Apologize." *Chicago Tribune*, September 12, 1937, B5.

———. "Record 46,572 See Dodgers Beat Cubs, 4–2." *Chicago Tribune*, May 19, 1947, 29.

Cahan, Richard, and Mark Jacob. *The Game That Was: The George Brace Baseball Photo Collection*. Chicago: Contemporary Books, 1996.

Churchill, Winston S. *Never Give In! The Best of Winston Churchill's Speeches*. New York: Hyperion, 2003.

Cohen, Robert. *The 50 Greatest Players in New York Yankees History*. Plymouth, UK: Scarecrow, 2012.

Daley, Arthur. "Sports of the Times: A Tragic Figure." *New York Times*, November 25, 1948, 52.

Dickens, Charles. *Great Expectations*. Hertfordshire, UK: Wordsworth Editions Limited, 2000.

Dickson, Paul. *Bill Veeck: Baseball's Greatest Maverick*. New York: Walker, 2012.

———. *The Dickson Baseball Dictionary*. 3rd ed. New York: Norton, 2009.

Dimnet, Ernest. *What We Live By*. New York: Simon & Schuster, 1932.

Display ad. *Chicago Tribune*, August 30, 1948, B3.

Durocher, Leo. *Nice Guys Finish Last*. With Ed Linn. Chicago: University of Chicago Press, 2009.

Ehrgott, Roberts. *Mr. Wrigley's Ball Club: Chicago and the Cubs During the Jazz Age*. Lincoln: University of Nebraska Press, 2013.

Eliot, T. S. *The Waste Land*. 1922. http://www.bartleby.com/201/1.html.

"Ernie Banks." BaseballLibrary.com. http://www.baseballlibrary.com/ballplayers/player.php?name=ernie_banks_1931.

"Famous Fans at Famous Battle Air Their Views." *Chicago Tribune*, September 23, 1927, 12.

Federal Baseball Club v. National League. 259 U.S. 200 (1922).

"Figures and Facts on the Fight Tonight." *Chicago Tribune*, September 22, 1927.

Fitzhenry, Robert I. *The Harper Book of Quotations.* 3rd ed. New York: HarperCollins, 1993.

Giamatti, A. Bartlett. *A Great and Glorious Game: Baseball Writings of A. Bartlett Giamatti.* Chapel Hill: Algonquin, 1998.

————. *Take Time for Paradise: Americans and Their Games.* New York: Bloomsbury USA, 1989.

Gibney, Alex. *Catching Hell.* ESPN Films, 2011.

Golenbock, Peter. *Wrigleyville: A Magical History Tour of the Chicago Cubs.* New York: St. Martin's Press, 1996.

Gordon, Dan, ed. *Your Brain on Cubs: Inside the Heads of Players and Fans.* New York: Dana, 2008.

Grossman, Ron. "'42' in the Windy City." *Chicago Tribune*, April 28, 2013.

Haupert, Michael. Correspondence with the author.

Hayner, Don, and Tom McNamee. *Streetwise Chicago: A History of Chicago Street Names.* Chicago: Loyola University Press, 1988.

Heaphy, Leslie A. *Black Baseball and Chicago: Essays on the Players, Teams and Games.* Jefferson, NC: McFarland, 2006.

Heinz, W. C. "Stan Musial's Last Day." *Life*, October 11, 1963.

Herzog, Bob. "Wilson's Record May Be the Most Awesome of All Time." *Los Angeles Times*, August 2, 1998. http://articles.latimes.com/1998/aug/02/sports/sp-9571.

Hettinger, Herman S. *A Decade of Radio Advertising.* Chicago: University of Chicago Press, 1933.

Hirdt, Steve. Correspondence with the author.

Ives, Martyn. *How Beer Saved the World.* Discovery Channel, 2011.

James, Bill. *The New Bill James Historical Baseball Abstract.* New York: Free Press, 2001.

Johnson, Steven. *The Ghost Map: The Story of London's Most Terrifying Epidemic—and How It Changed Science, Cities, and the Modern World.* New York: Riverhead, 2006.

Kepner, Tyler. "On a Sunny Day at Wrigley, a Perfect Storm of Offense." *New York Times,* May 17, 2009, SP1.

Krukow, Mike. Correspondence with the author.

A *League of Their Own.* Quotations are from the Internet Movie Database. http://www.imdb.com/title/tt0104694/quotes.

"Lee Elia Cubs Rant." Nuttysportsvideos. http://www.youtube .com/watch?v=8S0CDtEz_Bo.

Levine, Peter. A. G. *Spalding and the Rise of Baseball.* New York: Oxford University Press, 1985.

Lilienthal, David. *The Journals of David E. Lilienthal: The TVA Years, 1939–1945.* New York: Evanston, 1964.

Loverro, Thom. *Home of the Game: The Story of Camden Yards.* Dallas: Taylor, 1999.

Major League Baseball. http://mlb.mlb.com/home.

McCabe, Bret. "Janet Marie Smith Talks Ballparks and Urban Transformation." *Hub,* December 7, 2012. http://hub.jhu .edu/2012/12/07/berman-lecture-smith-ballparks.

McCollum, Dannel. "Champaign: The Creation of a City of Champaign." City of Champaign. http://ci.champaign.il.us/ about-champaign/history/creation-of-champaign/.

Montville, Leigh. *The Big Bam: The Life and Times of Babe Ruth.* New York: Doubleday, 2006.

Moreland, Keith. Correspondence with the author.

Moskowitz, Tobias J., and L. Jon Wertheim. *Scorecasting: The Hidden Influences Behind How Sports Are Played and Games Are Won.* New York: Crown Archetype, 2011.

Nathan, David H. *The McFarland Baseball Quotations Dictionary.* Jefferson, NC: McFarland, 2000.

Nidetz, Steve. "Despite Blowout in Game 1, Big Audience Got a Fine Show." *Chicago Tribune,* October 6, 1989.

Nightengale, Bob. "No Joy in Wrigleyville as Cubs, Neighbors Clash. *USA Today,* May 9, 2013.

"1929 World Series." Baseball-Reference.com. http://www.baseball-reference.com/bullpen/1929_World_Series.

Nolan, Martin F. "Advice to Red Sox: Just Keep Swinging." *Boston Globe,* September 1, 2001.

Okrent, Daniel. *Last Call: The Rise and Fall of Prohibition.* New York: Scribner, 2010.

O'Malley, Kathy, and Dorothy Collin. "Daleyville." *Chicago Tribune,* April 3, 1991.

O'Mara, Richard. "Like a Bat Out of Hell." *Baltimore Sun,* September 4, 1998. http://articles.baltimoresun.com/1998-09-04/features/1998247062_1_hack-wilson-baseball-robert/2.

Parker, Clifton Blue. *Fouled Away: The Baseball Tragedy of Hack Wilson.* Jefferson, NC: McFarland, 2000.

Reagan, Ronald. *An American Life: An Autobiography.* New York: Simon & Schuster, 1990.

Retrosheet: http://www.retrosheet.org/.

Ricketts, Tom. Correspondence with the author.

Royko, Mike. *One More Time: The Best of Mike Royko.* Chicago: University of Chicago Press, 1999.

Sandburg, Carl. *Chicago Poems.* 1916. http://www.bartleby.com/people/Sandburg.html.

———. *Smoke and Steel.* 1920. http://www.bartleby.com/people/Sandburg.html.

Sharrow, Ryan. "Power 20: Janet Marie Smith." *Baltimore Business Journal,* February 18, 2011. http://www.bizjournals.com/baltimore/print-edition/2011/02/18/power-20-janet-marie-smith.html?page=all.

Simon, Julian. *The Ultimate Resource 2.* Princeton: Princeton University Press, 1996.

Smith, Curt. *Pull Up a Chair: The Vin Scully Story*. Dulles, VA: Potomac Books, 2009.

Smith, Janet Marie. Correspondence with the author.

Society for American Baseball Research. http://sabr.org/research/.

Steele, Andrew. "Philip Wrigley." Society for American Baseball Research. http://sabr.org/bioproj/person/1043052b.

Stout, Glenn. *The Cubs: The Complete Story of Chicago Cubs Baseball*. New York: Houghton Mifflin, 2007.

Sullivan, Paul. Correspondence with the author.

"This Time It Will Be Better." *Desipio Blog*, October 1, 2007. http://www.desipio.com/?p=1390.

Thorn, John. *Baseball in the Garden of Eden: The Secret History of the Early Game*. New York: Simon & Schuster, 2011.

Towle, Mike. *Pete Rose: Baseball's Charlie Hustle*. Nashville: Cumberland House, 2003.

Tuttle, William M., Jr. "Contested Neighborhoods and Racial Violence: Prelude to the Chicago Riot of 1919." *Journal of Negro History*, vol. 55, no. 4 (October 1970), 266–88.

"2013 Official Baseball Rules: 2.00 Definition of Terms." Major League Baseball, 2013. http://mlb.mlb.com/mlb/downloads/y2013/official_baseball_rules.pdf.

Vaillancourt, Ryan. "Janet Marie Smith and the Changes to Dodger Stadium." *Los Angeles Downtown News*, February 12, 2013. http://www.ladowntownnews.com/news/janet-marie-smith-and-the-changes-to-dodger-stadium/article_41c5419e-7245-11e2-9350-0019bb2963f4.html.

Vecsey, George. *Stan Musial: An American Life*. New York: ESPN Books / Ballantine Books, 2011.

Veeck, Bill. *Veeck as in Wreck: The Autobiography of Bill Veeck*. With Ed Linn. Chicago: University of Chicago Press, 1962.

Weber, Bruce. "Ruth Ann Steinhagen Is Dead at 83; Shot a Ballplayer." *New York Times*, March 24, 2013, A22.

Wilentz, Sean. *The Best American History Essays on Lincoln*. New York: Palgrave Macmillan, 2009.

Will, George F. *Bunts: Curt Flood, Camden Yards, Pete Rose and Other Reflections on Baseball.* New York: Touchstone, 1999.

————. "Hooding Remarks." Princeton University, June 4, 2012. http://www.princeton.edu/main/news/archive/S33/88/44Q33/.

————. *"Your Brain on Cubs."* Newsweek, March 29, 2008.

Yellon, Al, Kasey Ignarski, and Matthew Silverman. *Cubs by the Numbers: A Complete Team History of the Chicago Cubs by Uniform.* New York: Skyhorse, 2009.

Zinsser, William. *The Writer Who Stayed.* Philadelphia: Paul Dry Books, 2012.

Text Credits

Photo Credits

Index

About the Author

GEORGE F. WILL is one of the most widely read writers in the world, with his twice-weekly syndicated column appearing in more than five hundred newspapers and online news sources. He is a Fox News contributor and the author of thirteen books, including *Men at Work, With a Happy Eye But . . .* , *Bunts, The Woven Figure,* and *One Man's America.* A winner of the Pulitzer Prize for Commentary and the Bradley Prize for outstanding intellectual achievement, he lives in Chevy Chase, Maryland.